T0255571

Lecture Notes in Computer Science 13737

Founding Editors

Gerhard Goos
Karlsruhe Institute of Technology, Karlsruhe, Germany

Juris Hartmanis
Cornell University, Ithaca, NY, USA

Editorial Board Members

Elisa Bertino
Purdue University, West Lafayette, IN, USA

Wen Gao
Peking University, Beijing, China

Bernhard Steffen
TU Dortmund University, Dortmund, Germany

Moti Yung
Columbia University, New York, NY, USA

More information about this series at https://link.springer.com/bookseries/558

Liang-Jie Zhang (Ed.)

Metaverse – METAVERSE 2022

18th International Conference
Held as Part of the Services Conference Federation, SCF 2022
Honolulu, HI, USA, December 10–14, 2022
Proceedings

Editor
Liang-Jie Zhang 🆔
Kingdee International Software
Group Co., Ltd.
Shenzhen, China

ISSN 0302-9743   ISSN 1611-3349 (electronic)
Lecture Notes in Computer Science
ISBN 978-3-031-23517-7   ISBN 978-3-031-23518-4 (eBook)
https://doi.org/10.1007/978-3-031-23518-4

© The Editor(s) (if applicable) and The Author(s), under exclusive license
to Springer Nature Switzerland AG 2022
This work is subject to copyright. All rights are reserved by the Publisher, whether the whole or part of the
material is concerned, specifically the rights of translation, reprinting, reuse of illustrations, recitation,
broadcasting, reproduction on microfilms or in any other physical way, and transmission or information
storage and retrieval, electronic adaptation, computer software, or by similar or dissimilar methodology now
known or hereafter developed.
The use of general descriptive names, registered names, trademarks, service marks, etc. in this publication
does not imply, even in the absence of a specific statement, that such names are exempt from the relevant
protective laws and regulations and therefore free for general use.
The publisher, the authors, and the editors are safe to assume that the advice and information in this book are
believed to be true and accurate at the date of publication. Neither the publisher nor the authors or the editors
give a warranty, expressed or implied, with respect to the material contained herein or for any errors or
omissions that may have been made. The publisher remains neutral with regard to jurisdictional claims in
published maps and institutional affiliations.

This Springer imprint is published by the registered company Springer Nature Switzerland AG
The registered company address is: Gewerbestrasse 11, 6330 Cham, Switzerland

Preface

To rapidly respond to the changing economy, the 2022 World Congress on Services (SERVICES 2022) naturally evolved to become the International Conference on Metaverse (METAVERSE 2022) to cover immersive services for all vertical industries and area solutions. We expect current services to be gradually transformed into immersive services that construct digital worlds and connect with physical worlds, and immersive services are the core characteristics of the Metaverse.

METAVERSE 2022 was one of the events of the Services Conference Federation event (SCF 2022), which had the following 10 collocated service-oriented sister conferences: the International Conference on Web Services (ICWS 2022), the International Conference on Cloud Computing (CLOUD 2022), the International Conference on Services Computing (SCC 2022), the International Conference on Big Data (BigData 2022), the International Conference on AI & Mobile Services (AIMS 2022), the International Conference on Metaverse (METAVERSE 2022), the International Conference on Internet of Things (ICIOT 2022), the International Conference on Cognitive Computing (ICCC 2022), the International Conference on Edge Computing (EDGE 2022), and the International Conference on Blockchain (ICBC 2022).

This volume presents the papers accepted at METAVERSE 2022. All topics related to metaverse engineering foundations and applications were considered, with a focus on novel approaches for engineering requirements, design, architecture, testing, maintenance and evolution, model-driven development, software processes, metrics, quality assurance and new software economics models, and search-based software engineering, enabling day-to-day services sectors and deriving from experience, with appreciation of scale, pragmatism, transparency, compliance, and dependability.

We accepted 10 papers, including 7 full papers and 3 short papers. Each was reviewed and selected by at least three independent members of the Program Committee. We are pleased to thank the authors whose submissions and participation made this conference possible. We also want to express our thanks to the Program Committee members for their dedication in helping to organize the conference and review the submissions. We owe special thanks to the keynote speakers for their impressive talks.

December 2022   Liang-Jie Zhang

Organization

Services Conference Federation (SCF 2022)

General Chairs

Ali Arsanjani	Google, USA
Wu Chou	Essenlix Corporation, USA

Coordinating Program Chair

Liang-Jie Zhang	Kingdee International Software Group, China

CFO and International Affairs Chair

Min Luo	Georgia Tech, USA

Operation Committee

Jing Zeng	China Gridcom, China
Yishuang Ning	Tsinghua University, China
Sheng He	Tsinghua University, China

Steering Committee

Calton Pu	Georgia Tech, USA
Liang-Jie Zhang	Kingdee International Software Group, China

SERVICES 2022

Program Chairs

Liang-Jie Zhang	Kingdee International Software Group, China

Program Committee

Chao Li	Beijing Jiaotong University, China
Xiuhua Li	Chongqing University, China
Xin Luo	Chongqing Institute of Green and Intelligent Technology, China
Waseem Mufti	Aalborg University Denmark
Sérgio Ribeiro	CPQD, Brazil

Stefano Sebastio	Raytheon Technologies, Ireland
Qi Chai	IoTeX, USA
Xinxin Fan	IoTeX, USA
Vikas Shah	Knights of Columbus, USA
Layth Sliman	EFREI- Paris, France
Zhu Xiangbo	Shenzhen Polytechnic, China
Kunjing Zhang	Institute of Information and Technology, China
Ben Falchuk	Peraton Labs, USA
Hasan Ali Khattak	National University of Sciences and Technology, Pakistan
Xiaohu Fan	Wuhan Collage, China

Services Society

The Services Society (S2) is a non-profit professional organization that was created to promote worldwide research and technical collaboration in services innovations among academia and industrial professionals. Its members are volunteers from industry and academia with common interests. S2 is registered in the USA as a "501(c) organization", which means that it is an American tax-exempt nonprofit organization. S2 collaborates with other professional organizations to sponsor or co-sponsor conferences and to promote an effective services curriculum in colleges and universities. S2 initiates and promotes a "Services University" program worldwide to bridge the gap between industrial needs and university instruction.

The Services Society has formed Special Interest Groups (SIGs) to support technology- and domain-specific professional activities:

- Special Interest Group on Web Services (SIG-WS)
- Special Interest Group on Services Computing (SIG-SC)
- Special Interest Group on Services Industry (SIG-SI)
- Special Interest Group on Big Data (SIG-BD)
- Special Interest Group on Cloud Computing (SIG-CLOUD)
- Special Interest Group on Artificial Intelligence (SIG-AI)
- Special Interest Group on Edge Computing (SIG-EC)
- Special Interest Group on Cognitive Computing (SIG-CC)
- Special Interest Group on Blockchain (SIG-BC)
- Special Interest Group on Internet of Things (SIG-IOT)
- Special Interest Group on Metaverse (SIG-Metaverse)

Services Conference Federation (SCF)

As the founding member of SCF, the first International Conference on Web Services (ICWS) was held in June 2003 in Las Vegas, USA. The First International Conference on Web Services - Europe 2003 (ICWS-Europe'03) was held in Germany in October 2003. ICWS-Europe'03 was an extended event of the 2003 International Conference on Web Services (ICWS 2003) in Europe. In 2004 ICWS-Europe changed to the European Conference on Web Services (ECOWS), which was held in Erfurt, Germany.

SCF 2019 was held successfully during June 25–30, 2019 in San Diego, USA. Affected by COVID-19, SCF 2020 was held online successfully during September 18–20, 2020, and SCF 2021 was held virtually during December 10–14, 2021.

Celebrating its 20-year birthday, the 2022 Services Conference Federation (SCF 2022, www.icws.org) was a hybrid conference with a physical onsite in Honolulu, Hawaii, USA, satellite sessions in Shenzhen, Guangdong, China, and also online sessions for those who could not attend onsite. All virtual conference presentations were given via prerecorded videos in December 10–14, 2022 through the BigMarker Video Broadcasting Platform: https://www.bigmarker.com/series/services-conference-federati/series_summit.

Just like SCF 2022, SCF 2023 will most likely be a hybrid conference with physical onsite and virtual sessions online, it will be held in September 2023.

To present a new format and to improve the impact of the conference, we are also planning an Automatic Webinar which will be presented by experts in various fields. All the invited talks will be given via prerecorded videos and will be broadcast in a live-like format recursively by two session channels during the conference period. Each invited talk will be converted into an on-demand webinar right after the conference.

In the past 19 years, the ICWS community has expanded from Web engineering innovations to scientific research for the whole services industry. Service delivery platforms have been expanded to mobile platforms, the Internet of Things, cloud computing, and edge computing. The services ecosystem has been enabled gradually, with value added and intelligence embedded through enabling technologies such as Big Data, artificial intelligence, and cognitive computing. In the coming years, all transactions involving multiple parties will be transformed to blockchain.

Based on technology trends and best practices in the field, the Services Conference Federation (SCF) will continue to serve as a forum for all services-related conferences. SCF 2022 defined the future of the new ABCDE (AI, Blockchain, Cloud, Big Data & IOT). We are very proud to announce that SCF 2023's 10 colocated theme topic conferences will all center around "services", while each will focus on exploring different themes (Web-based services, cloud-based services, Big Data-based services, services innovation lifecycles, AI-driven ubiquitous services, blockchain-driven trust service ecosystems, Metaverse services and applications, and emerging service-oriented technologies).

The 10 colocated SCF 2023 conferences will be sponsored by the Services Society, the world-leading not-for-profit organization dedicated to serving more than 30,000 services computing researchers and practitioners worldwide. A bigger platform means bigger opportunities for all volunteers, authors, and participants. Meanwhile, Springer will provide sponsorship for Best Paper Awards. All 10 conference proceedings of SCF 2023 will be published by Springer, and to date the SCF proceedings have been indexed in the ISI Conference Proceedings Citation Index (included in the Web of Science), the Engineering Index EI (Compendex and Inspec databases), DBLP, Google Scholar, IO-Port, MathSciNet, Scopus, and ZbMath.

SCF 2023 will continue to leverage the invented Conference Blockchain Model (CBM) to innovate the organizing practices for all 10 conferences. Senior researchers in the field are welcome to submit proposals to serve as CBM ambassadors for individual conferences.

SCF 2023 Events

The 2023 edition of the Services Conference Federation (SCF) will include 10 service-oriented conferences: ICWS, CLOUD, SCC, BigData Congress, AIMS, METAVERSE, ICIOT, EDGE, ICCC and ICBC.

The 2023 International Conference on Web Services (ICWS 2023, http://icws.org/2023) will be the flagship theme-topic conference for Web-centric services, enabling technologies and applications.

The 2023 International Conference on Cloud Computing (CLOUD 2023, http://thecloudcomputing.org/2023) will be the flagship theme-topic conference for resource sharing, utility-like usage models, IaaS, PaaS, and SaaS.

The 2023 International Conference on Big Data (BigData 2023, http://bigdatacongress.org/2023) will be the theme-topic conference for data sourcing, data processing, data analysis, data-driven decision-making, and data-centric applications.

The 2023 International Conference on Services Computing (SCC 2023, http://thescc.org/2023) will be the flagship theme-topic conference for leveraging the latest computing technologies to design, develop, deploy, operate, manage, modernize, and redesign business services.

The 2023 International Conference on AI & Mobile Services (AIMS 2023, http://ai1000.org/2023) will be a theme-topic conference for artificial intelligence, neural networks, machine learning, training data sets, AI scenarios, AI delivery channels, and AI supporting infrastructures, as well as mobile Internet services. AIMS will bring AI to mobile devices and other channels.

The 2023 International Conference on Metaverse (Metaverse 2023, http://www.metaverse1000.org/2023) will focus on innovations of the services industry, including financial services, education services, transportation services, energy services, government services, manufacturing services, consulting services, and other industry services.

The 2023 International Conference on Cognitive Computing (ICCC 2023, http://thecognitivecomputing.org/2023) will focus on leveraging the latest computing technologies to simulate, model, implement, and realize cognitive sensing and brain operating systems.

The 2023 International Conference on Internet of Things (ICIOT 2023, http://iciot.org/2023) will focus on the science, technology, and applications of IOT device innovations as well as IOT services in various solution scenarios.

The 2023 International Conference on Edge Computing (EDGE 2023, http://the edgecomputing.org/2023) will be a theme-topic conference for leveraging the latest computing technologies to enable localized device connections, edge gateways, edge applications, edge-cloud interactions, edge-user experiences, and edge business models.

The 2023 International Conference on Blockchain (ICBC 2023, http://blockc hain1000.org/2023) will concentrate on all aspects of blockchain, including digital currencies, distributed application development, industry-specific blockchains, public blockchains, community blockchains, private blockchains, blockchain-based services, and enabling technologies.

Contents

Research Track

Opportunities and Challenges in Metaverse the Rise of Digital Universe

Bharat S. Rawal[1](✉), Shakaib Ahmadand[2], Andrew Mentges[2], and Shami Fadli[2]

[1] Benedict College, Columbia, SC 29204, USA
bharat.rawal@benedict.edu
[2] Capitol Technology University, Laurel, MD 20708, USA

Abstract. The concept of the metaverse dates to 1992; however, the popularity of this concept has gained increased attention in 2021 following the announcement by Mark Zuckerberg. The topic of the metaverse is a new and attractive topic that is gaining increased insight from researchers. The paper focuses on a broader evaluation of the metaverse and web 3.0 technologies. Moreover, an assessment of the history and potential of these technologies is considered. Additionally, an evaluation of the available literature reviews between 1992 and 2022 was conducted. The assessment identified enormous attention on this scope from diverse multidisciplinary fields ranging from virtual reality, augmented reality, quantum communication, and blockchain. In the next ten years, expected progress is expected concerning metaverse and web 3.0 technologies. Consequently, these technologies will significantly impact how users interact with one another and how they associate with the internet. In this paper, we address the current security challenges and opportunities with the rise of the metaverse.

Keywords: Metaverse · Web 3.0 · Virtual reality · Internet · Quantum computing · AI/ML

1 Introduction

Since the introduction of the internet, dynamic advancements have been observed in cyberspace. These advancements have been observed in virtual technologies, social networking, video conferencing, and augmented reality applications, among others. Over recent years, increased attention has been placed on the advancement of virtual reality technologies, leading to the introduction of the metaverse. The word metaverse simply means "beyond this world" which comes from a combination of two words, the first word "meta" meaning "beyond" and the second word "universe" meaning "this world". Therefore, the term metaverse simply means "beyond this world." The term metaverse has attracted varying definitions in recent years. Decker & Peterson [1] define the metaverse as a computer-generated world that exists beyond the metaphysical and spiritual domains of the physical realm.

The metaverse concept has advanced since its introduction in 1992 and has attracted varying definitions. Irrespective, the metaverse concept is associated with inferences

© The Author(s), under exclusive license to Springer Nature Switzerland AG 2022
L.-J. Zhang (Ed.): METAVERSE 2022, LNCS 13737, pp. 3–17, 2022.
https://doi.org/10.1007/978-3-031-23518-4_1

by Neal Stephenson in 1992. In his novel Snow Crash, Stephenson, who developed the term metaverse, presented the metaverse based on a virtual world perspective [2]. Consequently, Stephenson considered the metaverse as a massive virtual environment that seeks to align with the physical world and at the same time allows users to interact as digital avatars. The introduction of this concept has attracted varying interpretations from diversified concepts over the decades. Dionisio et al. [2] explain that numerous studies have considered the metaverse as lifelogging, a collective space in virtuality, or the mirror world. Irrespective of these viewpoints, there is no concrete definition of the term.

The concept of the metaverse got little attraction and popularity in public over the last three decades. However, diverse inferences have been critical in advancing public knowledge on this concept. Decker & Peterson [1] explain that in 2018, the concept of Metaverse was presented in a project termed OASIS. The movie Ready Player One and the novel were based on the concept of project OASIS. This concept had enormous inference and was critical in advancing the concept's popularity. This concept was also applied in the Fortnite project and concerts where musicians such as Travis Scott and Ariana Grande held mega concerts.

The concept of metaverse attracted the most attention following the actions of Mark Zuckerberg, CEO of Facebook. In October 2021, Facebook announced its plan to change its name to Meta. The name change is marked to reflect the commitment of Zuckerberg to advancing the concept and the integration of the idea with Facebook. This action was further promoted by the company's increased investment in the metaverse. Following this announcement, public attention was drawn to the concept of the metaverse, attracting large companies, individuals, and states to the possibilities of the metaverse. According to Zuckerberg, the metaverse will serve as the next big computing platform compared to smartphone and mobile web development. The actions of Facebook marked an evolution aspect of the metaverse. Decker & Peterson [1] explain that increased Google search interest was experienced since the announcement.

On the other hand, major brands, and companies, including Google, Nike, Microsoft, gaming companies, and Tick-Tock, have explored ways of advancing the metaverse concept. It is essential to acknowledge that though there are numerous potentials associated with the metaverse, little inference has been developed. However, the concept has enormous potential, hence the need to identify possible adoptions of the metaverse in the future. Peterson [1] further notes that the future will be characterized by a shift from 2d to 3d metaverse applications. The application of the 3d metaverse is a concept under development; however, its establishment has not been realized, especially for large-scale usage. However, this concept may be available in the future. Further, the metaverse concept will connect the users and the brands, hence posing enormous inferences to product development processes note that the first paragraph of a section or subsection is not indented. The first paragraphs that follow a table, figure, equation, etc. do not have an indent (Fig. 1).

The following is how the rest of the paper is structured: The introduction is covered in section I, and the related work is covered in section II. Then, section III describes web 3.0. Section IV describes current approaches for known challenges. V explains the proposed solution. Section VI describes the metaverse in the age of quantum computing.

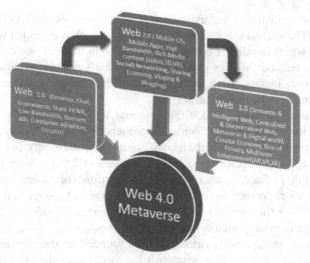

Fig. 1. Evolution of Metaverse.

Section VII talks about proficient multi-sided platforms and the security challenges of the metaverse. Section VIII describes the proposed architecture. Sections IX and X present analysis and discussion respectively. Finally, section XII concludes the research paper.

2 Related Works

Metaverse is a broad concept, attracting increased academic inferences in recent years. Over the past years, numerous studies have been established to seek and understand this concept. This section focuses on a range of related literature reviews that focus on the metaverse. One of the most insightful research projects was the Metaverse Roadmap which source to establish literature applicable in large systems of virtual environments. This study identified the Metaverse as a massive infrastructure that demanded the incorporation of interlinked virtual worlds. The establishment of this infrastructure is also required to transfer the internet from 2D to 3D.

These inferences were further advanced by the IEEE Virtual World group, which acknowledged that the establishment of the metaverse required was only possible from an individual virtual world. Dionisio et al. [2] explain that the progressive move from a particular world requires the establishment of separate worlds, commonly considered meta worlds. Over time and through technological advancement, an interconnected system is established, creating a hyper-grid or metagalaxies. Dionisio et al. [2] explain that metagalaxies are virtual environments that allow perceived teleportation from one region to another. This development eventually culminates in an entire metaverse composed of meta-galaxies and meta-world systems.

The metaverse essentially demands the integration of the duality of the physical and digital worlds. In achieving this duality, Leei et al. [6] explain that the metaverse must undergo diverse developments. The first development is the digital twins, which demands the inclusion of a high-fidelity digital model in the virtual scene. Consequently, the digital twins require for inclusion of factors such as temperature, motion, and functioning of diverse scopes. The second stage is the digital native, which is expected to be achieved through avatars which are digital creations that represent the real world. The third key stage is surrealistic and involves creating a setup that supports physical and virtual reality coexistence. Incorporating these stages will be critical; however, research on these applications is still at the infant stage.

The realization of a metaverse is still in progress, and the complete Implementation may take some time. Nevertheless, diverse researchers have sought to identify computational advances or critical factors in the advancement of virtual reality. In a study by Leei et al. [6], there are four key features essential in virtual world technology: psychological realism, the ubiquity of access, interoperability capabilities of content, and scalability. Psychological realism focuses on the ability of metaverse technology to transport a user from the physical to the virtual world. This scope demands both psychological and emotional engagement supported by the virtual environment.

The concept of an applicable virtual world is founded on the criteria that it offers an abundance of human interaction. Microsoft Research [8] explain that this concept is considered ubiquity and may be achieved through users' ability to transverse through the virtual environment while holding varying interactions with other users. On the other hand, this ubiquity demands the incorporation of perception factors in the virtual world similar to the physical world. Researchers also identified the critical relevance of interoperability infrastructure in the metaverse. These technologies essentially serve to enhance the ubiquity of the technology. This concept demands the inclusion of layered structures in technology, allowing users to interact irrespective of their physical differences.

The final scope identified in the research was scalability. According to Liu et al. [7], three scalability dimensions are vital in establishing the metaverse: concurrent avatars, scene complexity, and avatar interactions. The contemporary avatars demand that the metaverse hold many users interacting with each other. On the other hand, an efficient metaverse must ensure that the level of detail in the diverse scenes is complex, serving as a representation of the real world. The final aspect focused on the Avatar interactions and required the metaverse to accommodate a range of avatar interactions (Fig. 2).

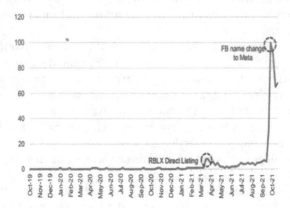

Fig. 2. Google Statistics following Metaverse mention by Facebook.

3   Challenges in WEB 3.0

The establishment of the metaverse is greatly dependent on the technological capability of transforming the internet from web 3.0. Web 3.0 essentially requires an integrated web where machines can efficiently interpret data. Web 3.0 will facilitate a word-wide data warehouse that allows for the sharing of data through any device or network. Web 3.0 is not confined to browsers or screens; instead, it is a web in a world of multi-devices, multi-channels, and metaverses. The theoretical presentation of Web 3.0 has attracted varying interpretations from diverse people resulting in disparity in opinions.

According to theorists, web 3.0 will be characterized by a range of challenges. Kreps & Kimppa [4] explain that one major challenge that will most likely be evident is the adoption process. Humans have failed to adopt certain technological initiatives throughout history due to fear of these devices. Therefore, there may be some form of resistance to adopting this technology. On the other hand, the adoption of web 3.0 will also face the challenge of privacy constraints. According to Kreps & Kimppa [4], web 3.0 is an advancement of web 2.0 characterized by significant privacy issues. Theorists have postulated that these challenges may be carried over into web 3.0.

As it exists presently, the internet is characterized by the presence of large chunks of information. Itinson [3] explains that the vastness of the internet poses enormous challenges to the implementation of web 3.0, and hence almost impossible to read these diverse semantics. On the other hand, the internet is considered vague, and therefore various queries are not specific and thus vague. Itinson [3] further notes the implementation of Web 3.0 is also faced with increased uncertainty which results in varying solutions. On the other hand, the internet is inconsistent and results from unreliable data (Fig. 3).

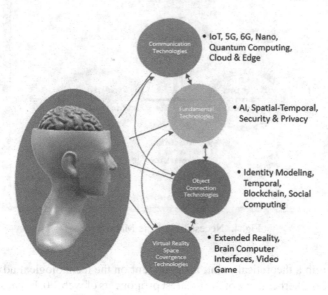

Fig. 3. Components of the Metaverse.

4   Approaches to Challenges

The establishment of Web 3.0 faces diverse challenges; however, various theoretical frameworks seek to offer solutions to these challenges. Kreps & Kimppa [4] explains that the challenges of Web 3.0 may be analyzed based on their key scopes; focus on technology, focus on social meaning, and public perception. The technological aspect was best retaliated by studies by Lassila and Hendler in 2007. Lassila & Hendler [5] explain that the existing challenges on Web 3.0 are founded on the wealth of data facing the internet. This concept has commonly been considered Big Data, critical in advancing the Internet of Things. Based on these inferences, it is essential to acknowledge that Web 3.0 is a semantic web technology that incorporates large web applications that significantly differ from the Internet of Things.

The establishment of Web 3.0, similar to the internet of things, has resulted in varying opinions. Consequently, diverse theorists have focused on this understanding, posing immense issues. Overcoming this challenge will demand an accurate knowledge of modern technology beyond this social network viewpoint. Kreps & Kimppa [4] note that the phenomenon has also been identified as a depiction of Web 2.0. Consequently, diverse scholars have acknowledged that there will be minor changes in web 3.0 culture. Based on these inferences, it is arguably based on the cultural construct of Web 2.0, which is immensely influenced by business rhetoric. This issue is prevalent, making it almost impossible to counter; however, there is a need for more understanding of the relevance of the technology (Fig. 4).

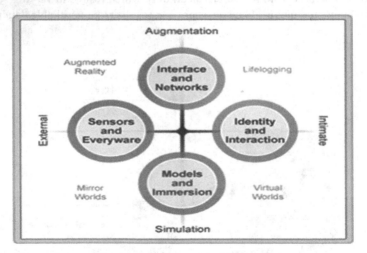

Fig. 4. Necessities of the Metaverse.

Web 3.0, from a theoretical point, is dependent on the technological advancements required. Mark Zuckerberg, one of the greatest proponents of web 3.0, has acknowledged that there is a need for increased improvement in technology to ensure that the technology is achieved. Moreover, it is estimated that the technology may take over ten years to accomplish due to the technological demands of the internet. This challenge is currently being addressed through increased involvement in research and technology development by significant organizations such as Meta, Google, and Microsoft, among others.

Web 2.0 has faced enormous challenges in terms of privacy. In a growing society characterized by technological advancement, privacy issues and threats to the internet continue to be prevalent issues. A majority of scholars have considerably associated this challenge with Web 3.0. The theoretical viewpoint on Web 3.0. Indicate that this technology will serve diverse roles, and hence privacy issues raise the greatest concern [4]. First, it is vital to acknowledge that web 3.0 is theoretical, and therefore there is insufficient knowledge to define how best the technology will function. Nevertheless, the internet has experienced growth in privacy policies and practices that seek to eliminate the challenge of privacy. Therefore, it is possible that following the establishment of the technology, these policies will be adopted to ensure privacy concerns are addressed on the new platform.

The final challenge identified relates to the vastness of internet 2.0 and the inability of modern technology to effectively make use of the available data to drive the required results. The vastness of the internet may, to the point, be most beneficial to the adoption of Web 3.0. First, web 3.0 requires enormous amounts of data to achieve, and this is easily achieved through the available data on the internet. Moreover, there is a need to integrate diverse scopes of the internet during the development of web 3.0 [5]. This advancement will be critical in ensuring that web 3.0 can wholly integrate the vast nature of the internet. On the other hand, web 3.0 seeks to create a broad network of web networks that can encompass these large data variables.

5 Proposed Solutions

The introduction of the Metaverse is characterized by the presence of varying challenges. One of the primary challenges that may be experienced relates to privacy threats. Privacy continues to be a prevalent challenge even with web 2.0. One critical aspect of privacy that will demand immediate attention relates to possible privacy leakages, raising varying concerns. Consequently, varying researchers have sought to define practical solutions to this issue. One recommended requirement for the redesigning of privacy criteria from the onset. This recommendation requires the developers to redesign privacy frameworks from scratch. Essentially, establishing these solutions will be critical in eliminating privacy concerns before they advance with time, posing greater challenges to Web 3.0.

About privacy, a growing concern has been raised over the collection of user information and their willingness to share the information posing a privacy paradox. As evidenced by web 2.0, most users have opted to share their information willingly, and the information collected is used to guide marketing practices [9]. Consequently, the advancement of Metaverse will demand the incorporation of modern technology that seeks to eliminate these challenges by adopting varying recommendations. One vital recommendation requires the absolute termination of user information-sharing mechanisms.

The technological advancement of the metaverse is expected to be guided by web 2.0, Consequently there is a likelihood that those systems will share numerous similarities. Researchers have hence sought to eliminate these challenges by establishing new cultures with innovative technology. Consequently, theorists have sought to pay increased focus on a range of interconnected challenges. Garon [9] explains that these challenges include user diversity, cyberbullying, fairness, and user addiction. First, it is crucial to acknowledge that with the adoption of recent technology, it is expected that these cultural challenges will most likely be experienced with the new technology. This creates the need to identify viable solutions that counter these challenges.

There are numerous viable solutions that theorists have focused on intending to eliminate these social challenges. The first recommendation demands the inclusion of algorithms that integrate easy detection of social challenges. Due to the dynamic technology to be adopted in the metaverse, scholars have urged the need to establish algorithms that can detect these social and unethical conduct. The second recommendation requires establishing strict policies that seek to reduce social threats associated with the adoption of the recent technology.

6 The Metaverse in the Age of Quantum Computing

Data is dramatically shaping the future of all humankind through algorithmic innovation, driving rapid advances in artificial intelligence, and bringing us closer to a safe and responsible Human-AI symbiosis. Over the last decade alone, the rapid proliferation of data and cognitive analytics enabled worldwide exponential growth for the digital economy, unlocking breakthrough scientific and technological advances and new market opportunities, virtually in every industry.

In digital marketing and advertising (AdTech), media agencies, marketers, and data publishers have harnessed customer PII and NON-PII data from CRM, behavioral data from connected devices, online and in-store commerce transactions, social media engagements, and audience intelligence from Search cloud platforms to better segment, target and run personalized, relevant and timely digital engagements and marketing campaigns that drive revenue conversion, audience reach, new customer acquisition and higher return on Ad Spend, leading to the rise of intelligent consumer-centric digital experiences and omnichannel commerce. Data is enabling retailers and brands worldwide to digitally transform at the edge. The industrial Internet of Things (IoT) supported by semiconductor, software, cloud, and telecommunication service providers, continue to enable more intelligent sensors, and connected devices, enabling consumers and enterprises that are moving to the edge to capture more data, analyze it faster, and automate actionable insights sooner.

Motivated by the consumer as the catalyst accelerator of this IoT industrial revolution, driving digital innovation and the exponential market expansion across every industry from integrated home automation, self-driving cars, integrated security surveillance, mesh networks, smart cities, smart hospitals, furthermore, creating more demand for faster compute, near-zero internet latency and more informed general artificial intelligence capabilities beyond classical binary-based cloud computing architecture.

In the defense industry, all domain awareness sensor data from the seabed to space is enabling defense agencies and military organizations across the services to develop new digital Joint All-Domain Command and Control (JADC2) capabilities.

As we enter this new era of human-machine symbiosis, accelerating the pace of the technological Darwinism evolution of Web 2.0 to one that enables the essential development of new cognitive digital concepts and experiences for the Metaverse, the data privacy and cybersecurity challenges remain a critical priority that must be addressed as they continue to evolve in variety and complexity.

7 Proficient Multi-sided Platform aND Security Challenges of Metaverse

Metaverse the coming age of technology would be widely available at a basic level, local electronic Security concern, and issued by the centralized server that must have several high-level features, such as confidentiality, resilience, scalability, and security. This division discusses design issues and the technical platform for Metaverse in the Coming Age of Technology.

7.1 Centralized and Distributed Models

Centralized or distributed services of many privately issued digital, data, such as Structured Data, Unstructured Data, and Semi-Structured Data rely on the blockchain or distributed computing technology to ensure that transactions are irreversible, it's natural to assume that. Centralized or Distributed services will do the same, as decentralized [13]. It might, however, be centralized digital data like nonlinear digital recovery data.

7.2 Immutability of Data Processing

The immutability of data processing is not an issue in a centralized data system since the system's state is confirmed by a central trustworthy party. Digital recovery data was created with the goal of achieving the Immutability of data processing in a decentralized setting without relying on a single authoritative entity. In the Metaverse the Coming Age of Technology, however, the central server is at least one trusted central party. As a result, many design elements would be unnecessary and undesirable. However, implementing them to a Coming Age of Technology would need further risk and difficulty assessments.

7.3 Availability and Resiliency of Data

Metaverse the coming age of technology that is widely available must have a prominent level of operational resilience. Due to its Digital Forensic for Web 3.0 structure, Web 3.0 offers this benefit over centralized systems, which suffer from employs point of failure. Web 3.0 Ontology that employs Ontology can continue to operate without interruption even if one of the Web 3.0 Ontologies fails or the central server goes down for a period of time. This is the key distinction from the current centralized system. However, this Quantum Computing on Web 3.0 robustness is not required in all scenarios. For instance, when all nodes are running the same defective code, the system will shut down. To achieve high resilience, centralized systems might use numerous backups. However, Quantum Computing on Web3 has the ability to improve efficiency and cost-effectiveness while also increasing resilience.

7.4 Security and Privacy Concerns

The system of Security and Privacy concerns must allow different parties to assist verify data in order to provide full resilience and security advantages. However, this threatens data privacy since others will have access to secure data. Quantum Computing on Web 3.0 systems still have privacy difficulties since they use pseudonyms or addresses instead of real-world identities. Hackers can deduce various facts by examining pseudonyms or addresses, according to many researchers. As a result, this does not provide genuine privacy. Instead, consider the following basic techniques to dealing with Quantum Computing on Web 3.0 privacy: Permissioned distributed ledger technology, no sensitive data on the shared ledger, data encryption, and cryptographic protocols like Zero-knowledge proof.

7.5 Operation Efficiency Write the Scalability

Today's distributed Operation of Scalability gives the Efficiency for example, must scale to satisfy the demand of data confirmation in a high peak load of thousands of data processing per second, which takes roughly few minutes for data processing and around 15 s for unsecure process. However, according to the most recent research study, it enables significant throughput, up to 100,000 data processing per second. More data processing will increase the number of data validation relative to existing data verification systems for utilizing the resources. To deal with this, Operation Efficiency write the Scalability will have to determine whether to enhance their computer operational capacity.

To encounter proficient multi-sided platforms and security challenges of the metaverse, the following privacy Coe rations are enabled by the security feature in quantum computing on web 3.0.

7.6 Quantum Communication Models

Quantum communication is among the most fascinating concepts that seek to exploit the quantum nature of the information. One of the key scopes of the quantum communication modes seeks to encompass fundamentally new computer science solutions that exceed classical communication systems. Quantum communication systems are considered critical as they offer absolute randomness and absolute security and can manage larger amounts of information compared to traditional classical binary operations.

The quantum communication models are expected to revolutionize the contexts of the metaverse completely. First, quantum communication channels will offer a broader stage for the establishment of the metaverse. Further, these channels advance on the 5G and 6G environments, allowing for increased security. Gyongyosi et al. [12] explain that quantum communication enhances the metaverse by using quantum key bases that are evidenced in the quantum non-cloning theorem and uncertainty principles. The abilities of quantum communications are further emphasized by the superposition properties of the qubits (Fig. 5).

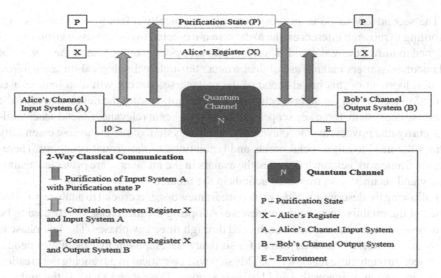

Fig. 5. Quantum Communication Models.

8   Proposed Framework

The scope of the metaverse may be considered to encompass unique interdisciplinary aspects. Consequently, the proposed framework on the metaverse has been linked to over ten key scopes that are considered significantly important in the actualization of the metaverse dream. Consequently, diverse scholars have attributed the frameworks based on two major categories: ecosystem and technology. Essentially, these two scopes are interconnected, and this means that the adoption of the metaverse will demand the inclusion of these scopes. Further Liu et al., [7] explain that this interconnectedness is understood by considering technological adoption as the architectural support of the metaverse while the ecosystem is the gigantic application of the metaverse. Based on the scope of this essay, this proposed framework also acknowledges the need for both technological and ecosystem systems during the development of the metaverse.

One of the critical categories vital in establishing the metaverse is the technological scope. Based on available statistics, eight key pillars will be fundamental during the development of the metaverse. First, the extended reality and user interactivity technologies will be critical in defining how diverse users will access the metaverse. These scopes will further define how many users have access to the metaverse at one given moment. The second key pillar will include technologies that define how users interact with the metaverse and the XR. These key technological adoptions will include computer visions, artificial intelligence, blockchains, and the Internet of things. The third scope of the technological adoption will focus on the performance of the metaverse, which will be supported through edge computing techniques. Edge computing and cloud-based computing systems have significant relevance in data processing and massive computational capabilities. These systems in the metaverse will serve to enhance the application performance, storage, and user experiences.

The second key scope is an ecosystem which typically refers to the virtual world. According to research inferences, the metaverse is expected to encompass a virtual world designed to mirror the real world. Therefore, the ecosystem component of the metaverse will encompass users making use of their avatars through technological infrastructures. The development of this broad scope of the metaverse concept will also require user interaction techniques for diverse activities and content. During the development of the metaverse ecosystem, three key scopes will be of significant relevance: social acceptability, security and privacy, and accountability. The ecosystem of the metaverse essentially dictates the need to align social norms and regulations to the virtual economy. Therefore, the framework acknowledges that the avatars in the metaverse are protected against privacy and security risks over their actions in the metaverse.

Following the description of the metaverse framework, it is crucial to analyze possible phases in the establishment of the metaverse. Adopting the metaverse is expected to be a progressive endeavor that will be achieved through three key phases. The first phase is the social metaverse, which advocates for software development that facilitates people to connect through these meta worlds. This step will be critical in advancing the creation and incorporation of innovative and business scopes. The second phase is the ambient metaverse which is expected to offer a connection to the social metaverse that goes beyond the scope of mobile devices. This phase will demand the inclusion of new devices that will allow access into the metaverse through any form of the screen surface. The final phase is considered to be the singularity metaverse which will only be achieved through hyper-connectivity. This scope is considered to be the final stage of the singularity and will encompass the entire adoption of the diverse technological scopes of the metaverse framework indicated above.

9 Architecture

The scope of the metaverse is significantly expected to be grounded in the virtual world. The virtual world (VW) has been identified as an architectural design for which the metaverse will be established and designed as an extension of the real world. The architectural development of the metaverse has been a fascinating concept that has best been reflected in diverse movies. Archiving this architectural design will demand the development of a digital environment that encompasses our real world's physical appearance and maintains cultural, social, and philosophical interactions. The architecture of the metaverse is not a new concept; rather, it is a concept that has been advanced by scopes in virtual reality and the gaming sector. Realizing this architecture based on the frameworks advanced in this context, the architecture of the metaverse will demand major adoptions.

One of the key adoptions is founded on integrating a digital spatial revolution. Liu et al., [7] explain that traditional virtual environments have been limited, creating the need for architectures to go beyond realism in virtual environments. This architectural adoption will require increased virtual world creativity by abandoning depictions of reality and giving mindfulness to out-of-this-world designs. It is crucial to acknowledge that the relevance of the metaverse design is to establish a reality that allows the impossible to be possible. Second, the architectural development process must acknowledge the fact that the development of the metaverse demands dynamic interactive processes between users and the metaverse. This is achievable following the understanding that striking disparities exist between the metaverse and the virtual reality scopes (Fig. 6).

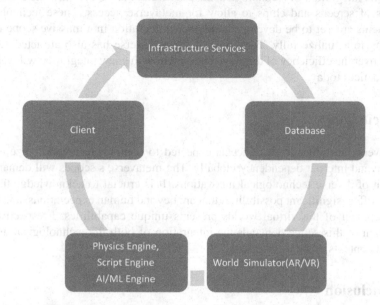

Fig. 6. The AI/ML-centric architecture used in virtual worlds

The metaverse design will also demand integrating key user information and scopes, including their histories, into the design of the virtual world. Liu et al., [7] explain that one of the key characteristics of the metaverse is that the virtual world is timeless. This creates the need to incorporate historical information during the architectural design of the metaverse. Moreover, the architectural design must incorporate state-of-the-art computer modeling and animations that may adopt 2D or 3D designs. The 3D designs must be integrative and interactive encompassing visual art and technology that focus on the landscape, urban planning, and avatar designs.

10   Analytical Analysis

The metaverse is a digital universe beyond the internet scopes we currently use today. The vision of the future state of the web poses significant possibilities evidenced by the transformation in social interaction, business, and the internet economy. The scope of the metaverse, however, is subject to increased inferences. First, web 3.0 network development is not easy, and its ultimate adoption is expected to be achieved by 2047. Irrespective, enormous steps have been adopted in recent years, with the past year experiencing increased academic research inferences in this scope.

Due to the dynamic nature of the metaverse, it is crucial to critically analyze the metaverse's scope. First, at the basic level, the metaverse entails the integration of diverse key scopes in enhancing the efficiency of these systems. Irrespective, it is crucial to acknowledge the challenge that exists in the ultimate integration of these diverse pillars to the ultimate establishment of the metaverse. Moreover, the development of the metaverse demands the integration of technological adoptions that may encompass the creation of new types of screens and chips to allow for metaverse access. These technological advancements are yet to be developed, and their integration in a massive scope is still challenging to actualize fully. The scope of the metaverse has also attracted varying criticisms over the efficiency of these systems and how the new integration will enhance current practices today.

11 Discussion

The metaverse introduces new concepts expected to completely revolutionize human interaction and internet dependency globally. The metaverse's scopes will demand the integration of diverse technological innovations. It is crucial to acknowledge that the metaverse offers significant possibilities that are beyond human expectations, and hence the development of the virtual worlds presents unique capabilities. Irrespective, the actualization of this scope demands the integration of both the technological and the ecological contexts.

12 Conclusion

The metaverse and Web 3.0 pose significant technological potential in the future. Nevertheless, these advancements in this scope greatly depend on the effective adoption of technology and innovation. Numerous trends have been experienced since the introduction of the internet and the integration of diverse infrastructures such as web 2.0, the internet of things, and the virtual reality concept. Throughout this research, various scholars have aimed at establishing viable frameworks critical to the establishment of the Metaverse. Nevertheless, few descriptive and comprehensive studies focus on the subject. This shortage in literature may be associated with the fact that there in the past, there was little emphasis on this subject.

Over the past years, there has been an increase in literature on the scope. However, there is an enormous disparity in these fields and a lack of a unison framework that guides the establishment of the metaverse and the wen 3.0. There, however, exists massive potential in this technological innovation and hence the need to establish solutions that seek to combat the existing challenges.

References

1. Decker, P.D.D., Peterson, S.P.: Beyond Virtual or Physical Environments. A White Paper for NDRIO's Canadian Digital Research Needs Assessment (2021)
2. Dionisio, J.D.N., Burns, G.B., III, Gilbert, R.: 3D Virtual Worlds and the metaverse. ACM Computing Surveys **45**(3), 1–38 (2013). https://doi.org/10.1145/2480741.2480751

3. Itinson, K.: WEB 1.0, WEB 2.0, Web 3.0: stages of development of web technologies and their impact on education. Karelian Scientific Journal **9**(30) (2020). https://doi.org/10.26140/knz4-2020-0901-0005
4. Kreps, D., Kimppa, K.: Theorizing Web 3.0: ICTs in a changing society. Information Technology & People **28**(4), 726–741 (2015). https://doi.org/10.1108/itp-09-2015-0223
5. Lassila, O., Hendler, J.: Embracing Web 3.0. IEEE Internet Computing **11**(3), 90–93 (2007). https://doi.org/10.1109/mic.2007.52
6. Leei, L.-H.L., et al.: All one needs to know about metaverse: a complete survey on technological singularity, virtual ecosystem, and research agenda. Journal of Latex **14**(8), 1–61 (2021)
7. Liu, H., Bowman, M., Adams, R., Hurliman, J., Lake, D.: Scaling virtual worlds: Simulation requirements and challenges. In: Proceedings of the Winter Simulation Conference (WSC). The WSC Foundation, Baltimore, MD, pp. 778–790 (2010)
8. Microsoft Research: (2021, October 13). ISMAR 2021 Keynote 1: Mar Gonzalez Franco - Metaverse from Fiction to Reality and the Research Behind It. https://www.microsoft.com/en-us/research/video/keynote-1-mar-gonzalez-franco-metaverse-from-fiction-to-reality-and-the-research-behind-it/
9. Garon, J.M.: Legal Implications of a Ubiquitous Metaverse and a Web3 Future. SSRN Electron. J. (2022). https://doi.org/10.2139/ssrn.4002551
10. Smart, J.M., Cascio, J., Paffendorf, J.: Metaverse Roadmap Overview (2007)
11. Gyongyosi, L., Imre, S., Nguyen, H.V.: A Survey on Quantum Channel Capacities. IEEE Communications Surveys & Tutorials **20**(2), 1149–1205 (2018). https://doi.org/10.1109/comst.2017.2786748
12. Hunter, M.: Defi100 claims website Hack was behind Exit Scam message. FullyCrypto (24 May 2021). [Online]. Available: https://fullycrypto.com/defi100-claims-website-hack-was-behind-exit-scam-message. Accessed: 11 Mar 2022
13. Moon, U.-K., Huang, G.: CMOS implementation of nonlinear spectral-line timing recovery in digital data-communication systems. IEEE Trans. Circuits Syst. I Regul. Pap. **51**(2), 298–308 (2004). https://doi.org/10.1109/TCSI.2003.822395. Feb

Exploration of Short Video Media Communication Based in the Metaverse

Chunyan Jiang and Jinhong Xu[⊠]

ShenZhen Institute of Information Technology, ShenZhen 518172, China
3383199759@qq.com

Abstract. As media is embedded in human daily life, human society has experienced two stages of face-to-face unmediated real communication and virtual world, and is ushering in the metaverse communication in the era of deep media. Metaverse, as the dominance of the era of deep media communication, media forms is constantly generated. Different from the previous media, it allows human beings to "enter" through various terminals to experience and act. It is a kind of "experiential" media. It breaks through the traditional concept of using short video media information as a carrier and tool for communication. It constitutes the infrastructure of the future human society. It is a "survival" medium. The metaverse promotes the deep metaverse of daily life at the material, spiritual and social levels, providing a new possibility for future human society, work and life. The arrival of the metaverse era will realize the multi-dimensional and multi-modal ecological application of diversity, multi-scenario, multi-industry and multi-energy when human beings face short video media dissemination.

Keywords: Metaverse · Short Video · Media · Communication

1 Background

The Metaverse is a "new invention" embedded in the sequence of digital revolution and Internet technology development. With the rapid development of internet companies and the acceleration of global information flow, both are breeding grounds for media communication. Metaverse restores the mainstream media that once dominated human society to secondary media and subordinate media. The most representative domestic and foreign media, Tik Tok (中国抖音) is prevalent at the moment. In 2021, Tik Tok will surpass Facebook in app store downloads and become the most downloaded app in the world. "New York Times" columnist Sheila Ovid pointed out: "Tik Tok is providing the next generation of activists with a new way of storytelling and challenging the global Internet order." As the most successful domestic, international short film in recent years one of the cases of video media communication, Douyin takes the platform rather than the content as the logic, builds a platform ecosystem on an international scale, and obtains control over content communication. Since the 21st century, the "GAFAM" (Google, Amazon, Facebook, Apple, Microsoft) system in the United States has been leading the world, while the "BAT" (Baidu, Alibaba, Tencent) system in China has dominated

© The Author(s), under exclusive license to Springer Nature Switzerland AG 2022
L.-J. Zhang (Ed.): METAVERSE 2022, LNCS 13737, pp. 18–28, 2022.
https://doi.org/10.1007/978-3-031-23518-4_2

China. The dissemination path of short video media. Especially under the prevailing conditions of the metaverse, the effective combination of virtual world and real life is vividly reflected in the short video media, which also provides a solid foundation for the communication medium of the metaverse. The overall architecture of this paper is mainly reflected in Fig. 1.

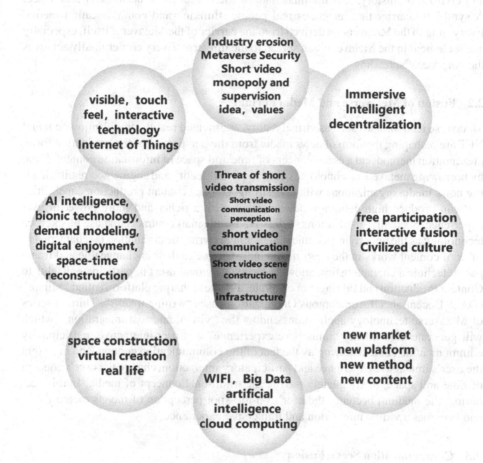

Fig. 1. Metaverse + Communication integration diagram

2 Fusion of the Metaverse and Communication

2.1 The Metaverse is a Vehicle that Integrates People and Media

In the academic field of journalism and communication, many scholars have conducted theoretical research on the original works from the perspective of the media. Scholars believe that the Metaverse is the latest wave of the Internet technology, communication revolution, and it is also the third wave. It is a fusion of the present and the expected or the future. The ultimate communication medium for all inclusive technologies. The original universe builds a larger universe that integrates the natural universe and the real universe through diverse and inclusive digital technologies and various aspects of content. It is an advanced form of cyberspace (version 2.0) with characteristics such as high fidelity, virtual-real interaction and embodied immersion history, free participation, integration and civilization history. It is the final state of the evolution of network virtual space. A symbiotic carrier that integrates real people, thinking and communication media. Everything in the Metaverse is derived from the carrier of the Metaverse itself, especially every element in the Metaverse can spread to the universe. Every corner finally achieves the purpose of spreading.

2.2 Fusion of Metaverse and Media Format

Metaverse technologies such as virtual reality, augmented reality, digital enjoyment and NFT are reshaping the form of news media from the perspective of the production form, presentation method and a user's concept of time and space of information content. First, by borrowing metaverse technologies such as virtual reality and augmented reality, leading news media organizations will have stronger visual content production capabilities and can produce high-definition news content with a richer and more powerful user experience. Secondly, applications such as NFT and smart contracts that use blockchain technology as the underlying technical logic may rewrite the circulation mechanism and rules of content works in the news media industry due to their unchangeable and transparent technical characteristics, allowing more individual users to participate. Rights to Content Production and Editing. For example, a content sharing platform called "Mirror" (DAO, Decentralized Autonomous Organization) uses "writing tokens". Third, a series of Metaverse technology applications endow the "virtual and real integration", which will generate high-fidelity "immersive experience" and user-interactive, participatory communication content, downplay the fact of the communication content, and highlight the user's immersive experience and participatory interaction, change the user's concept of time and space, or completely rewrite the traditional concept of media. In this scenario, "the medium becomes the user's on-the-spot perception of reconstructed facts" and becomes a virtual interaction and immersive experience.

2.3 Communication Scene Fusion

The fusion of reality and reality and the reconstruction of time and space are the core propositions in the concept of the metaverse. The fusion of reality and reality is the external presentation of the metaverse, while the reconstruction of time and space is an implicit feature. The connection between time and space is broken, thus presenting a rich and diverse scene. On the two levels of time and space, multiple superimposed scenes can be presented, such as scenes from the past are presented in the future, and scenes from other places are presented here. Entering the initial stage of development, this scenario is actually more about somatosensory and communication, which provides a practical place for the user's body to enter the communication field in the post-human era. As an all-real shared space that provides users with an immersive interactive experience, the Metaverse is precisely creating a social scene of "coexistence" that meets the needs of both parties, placing interpersonal and human-computer interaction at the core of the scene, and is short-term. Video media communication provides the necessary basic environment and scenes.

2.4 Fusion of Communication Perception

Metaverse, as a new application form of the organic integration of various Internet elements, will promote the deep involvement of the human body and mind in communication, while embodied communication emphasizes the interaction of mind, body and environment. Peters said, "The body is not a carrier that can be discarded. In a sense, the body is the homeland we are returning to." In recent years, emerging technologies such as VR/AR/MR, interactive technology, artificial intelligence, cloud computing, and Internet of Things technology to develop rapidly. Their application in the field of information dissemination constantly drives humans to simulate, simulate and even recreate the daily interaction between their minds, bodies and the environment, bringing human voice, touch, limbs and other organs into the communication process, making immersive communication from Imagination moves towards reality, further highlighting the importance of the body in the communication process. Interaction technologies such as VR/AR/MR realize the embedded interaction between the user's virtual body, cognitive system and virtual scene. Sensors placed on the body can transmit the brain's instructions to the body, combining the real body with the virtual body, which can be "get" or "see, hear, touch".

3 Characteristics of Propagation in the Metaverse Context

The Metaverse is not only the product of the current media society's development to the stage of "deep media", but also an important dynamic mechanism for promoting all-round in-depth media. Its final form will be to achieve a high degree of integration of the physical world, virtual world and human society, and then reconstruct the material ecology, social ecology and spiritual ecology of human society, thus becoming the latest feature of human living conditions in the future.

3.1 Characteristics of Immersive Experience Communication

Metauniverse, as an all-real Internet space that provides users with an immersive interactive experience, just creates a "coexistence" social scene for users that meets the needs of both parties, and puts interpersonal and human-computer interaction at the core of the scene. The breakthrough for the metaverse is immersive content. The degree of fusion between immersive virtual content (such as games, anime, etc.) as the concept of the metaverse develops and permeates.) and immersive physical content (such as media, social, film and television, etc.) will be higher and higher. In other words, the "hyperuniverse" will play a bigger role as a medium. The Metaverse is a virtual world that is seamlessly connected to the real society and synchronized with the same frequency. As the dominant media form of human social interaction in the deep media era, the metaverse will inevitably reconstruct the ecology of human social interaction. Therefore, the interpersonal relationships in the metaverse are also the sum of real interpersonal relationships, virtual interpersonal relationships, and virtual reality interpersonal relationships. It not only liberates human social communication from face-to-face communication without intermediary and virtual communication with intermediary, and forms digital communication with intermediary, but also can connect virtual and reality, and reconstruct the space and communication experience of human social communication. As an infrastructure-based medium for the survival of human society in the future, the Metaverse can promote the deep medium of human society at the material, spiritual and social levels, thus becoming a media infrastructure for human beings to engage in the material, spiritual and social interactions, providing human social interactions. A whole new space.

3.2 Intelligent Communication Form

The development of the universe provides a more integrated application space for new technology, media such as artificial intelligence, virtual reality, blockchain, and big data, and promotes the iterative upgrade of traditional media. Artificial anchors are virtual intelligent media products. They are responsible for hosting and broadcasting news reports on radio, television, and the Internet, and have gone through a series of iterative processes such as TV anchors, virtual anchors of video websites, and AI synthetic anchors. In 2000, the United Kingdom first introduced the virtual host "Ananova" in online video programs. She reported the news in place of the live anchor, rarely made mistakes, and did not need a break, so she was welcomed by the TV station. In 2018, Xinhua News Agency launched the world's first AI composite anchor, using the voice, smile and broadcast material of CCTV host Qiu Hao as the original data. With the help of artificial intelligence technology, "Xin Xiaohao" can not only broadcast news, but also conduct simple interactions based on audience feedback, and has certain interpersonal skills. Following the breakthrough and innovation of Xinhua News Agency, on May 25, 2019, People's Daily launched the first artificial intelligence virtual anchor to realize multilingual automatic news broadcast. After that, CCTV launched virtual anchors "Kang Xiaohui", "Xiao Sa", "Zhu Xiaoxun" and so on. These AI anchors enrich the look and form of news reports with their unique charisma and image. After that, local media closely followed the pace of central media and increased investment in intelligent media products such as artificial intelligence anchors. People's familiarity with the human-computer interaction of virtual idols and virtual anchors is also conducive to improving their acceptance of virtual digital assets, and they are willing to pay for virtual characters in the virtual world, such as buying tickets to participate in virtual characters' concerts, etc. Build the underlying economic system of the Metaverse.

3.3 Features of Decentralized Propagation

The influence of the universe on the transformation and development of media is also reflected in "decentralization". The future super universe will be a world of billions or even more people, and it cannot be completed by a few, dozens, or hundreds of organizations. Some researchers believe that the essence of the media evolution from the "scenario age" to the "metaverse" to the "spiritual world" is to help people break through the existing limitations and break through the "extension of the human body" in the outward and inward directions. Degrees of freedom. At the same time, the complexity, accuracy and timeliness of information release will be further improved. From the perspective of propagation accuracy, the big data network composed of big data, cloud computing, edge computing and algorithms will help to store data, analyze the relationship of information and process user portraits. Accordingly, the media itself can portray dynamic and accurate user portraits. The combination of the two will greatly improve the accuracy of user information dissemination. From the perspective of the timeliness of distribution, the cloud-based metaverse trend makes it possible to implement edge computing, thus saving time for data transmission. High-speed and low-latency 5G communication technology and intelligent automatic artificial intelligence technology can not only solve the transmission delay and sensory dizziness problems of multi-modal information in VR/AR/MR applications, but also can calculate the massive data of user communication activities, Storage, rendering, and processing are moved to the cloud, increasing the intelligence of the metaverse and the timeliness of delivery.

4 Video Media Transmission Path Based on Metaverse Perspective

4.1 Improve the Diversification, Multi-Dimensionality and Diversity of Short Video Dissemination

Metaverse promotes the integrated development of short video media communication. The development of short video media has been in development for a period of time, and it has also achieved certain results. A series of digital technologies in Metaverse have a transformative impact on video creation, user experience, etc. Some scholars have described the importance of planning and deploying the application of short video media Metaverse. In the process of using metaverse technology to spread diverse short video media, first of all, it is necessary to make corresponding ideological settings. Because short video media has a large spread effect and a widespread range, if there is a problem with ideological orientation, then it will definitely be a disaster, so we must carry out certain constraints and restrictions in thinking, and actively promote excellent, high-quality, cultural, breath, content, and connotative related content; Secondly, we must focus on short In the design and formulation of video content, not all forms of communication can be directly displayed to the mass media. Certain settings and technical processing are required, and virtual projection technology, 4D imaging and other means are used to help users obtain visual, auditory, tactile, and olfactory senses. All-round experience. In the process of short video content dissemination, it is necessary to remember the diversification of content, multi-dimensionality, and diversity are divided from the level of the public, from the needs of college and high school education, social needs, national needs, and regional divisions to continuously derive targeted a metaverse of sexual and widely distributed short videos.

4.2 Expand New Markets for Short Video Media Communication

Using Metaverse technology to enhance the interactivity of short video media dissemination in online and offline linkage, let high-quality short video content speaks for itself, the Metaverse of short video media shows its eternal charm on the basis of displaying audio-visual content. For example, in the use of metaverse to spread intangible cultural heritage, the production process of traditional skills is artistic. Although it can be expressed in words at this time, the process of audio-visual presentation allows the audience to discover more artistic charms that were originally overlooked in the intuitive appreciation, and these contents are all art worthy of being recorded. It is necessary to combine the VR panoramic immersive communication mode to break through the limitations of time and space, especially for the dissemination of intangible cultural heritage. As a comprehensive cultural communication activity that integrates art appreciation, product production, and local customs, the immersive experience can make the audience truly feel the atmosphere and charm of traditional culture, and further expand new markets.

4.3 Expand a New Platform for Short Video Media Communication

Expanding a new platform for short video media communication is a very important management activity. At present, there are many short video platforms, but relatively few are relatively complete. In the process of short video media communication, the focus is on the content. The construction of the other aspects is relatively weak. For example, it is necessary to focus on building a platform strategic management department, setting up a media development department of metaverse Universe, so that short video content can promote media innovation and content change through media censorship or overall planning capabilities. Jung et al. (2022) study proposed several improvement measures to upgrade makerspace as a digital conversion platform. In particular, it is necessary to strengthen the values of supervision and core departments, the world outlook and the outlook on life, and realize the real meaning of short video content and the spread of the universe. In particular, combining the advantages of circular universe technology and big data analysis and algorithmic scenarios to distinguish the public, the combined and preferred source universe short media dissemination content enhances the promotion, effectiveness and guiding role of short video media.

4.4 Enrich the Content of Short Video Media

Expanding a new platform for short video media communication is a very important management activity. At present, there are many short video platforms, but relatively few are relatively complete. In the process of short video media communication, the focus is on the content. The construction of the other aspects is relatively weak. For example, it is necessary to focus on building a platform strategic management department, setting up a media development department of metaverse Universe, so that short video content can promote media innovation and content change through media censorship or overall planning capabilities. In particular, it is necessary to strengthen the values of supervision and core departments, the world outlook and the outlook on life, and realize the real meaning of short video content and the spread of the universe. In particular, combining the advantages of circular universe technology and big data analysis and algorithmic scenarios to distinguish the public, the combined and preferred source universe short media dissemination content enhances the promotion, effectiveness and guiding role of short video media.

5 Potential Threat of Short Video Transmission in the Metaverse

Just as the law of the development of things is a spiral upward and a wavelike advance, since entering the post-epidemic era, the short video industry has encountered unprecedented development opportunities in the process of progress, and is also trapped in the barriers to break through. Judging from the current dynamic development trend of the industry, the short video industry is facing a series of difficulties such as content creation, regulatory mechanisms, and sustainable development.

5.1 Erosion in Some Industries

Metaverse short video dissemination will have its own advantages, and it will also impact a series of other activities. With the improvement of new business models such as ecological technology, economic policy and strategic guidelines, the dissemination of short videos will inevitably cause other departments or institutions to fall into operational difficulties, especially under the new round of impact from the Metaverse, new Under a round of changes, short video dissemination will not only affect its own industry, but also other industries, such as the advertising industry, financial industry, knowledge industry, radio and nightclub business, etc. These are all traditional industries in the past, but in the short-term after the emerging video media broke out, their original business industries and economic business models have changed. Whether these problems can be solved during the dissemination of Metaverse short videos, or whether there is any effective way to control them, is unknown. Only by grasping the current development status and making assumptions about future expectations, laying out and cultivating new businesses and optimizing business models in advance, and generating a cycle of new industrial chains, can we actively integrate into the development process of Metaverse and avoid the industry being affected by The impact of the short video dissemination of the language universe, but there is no way to change the revitalization industry.

5.2 Metaverse Security

Whether the metaverse can lead to a better digital civilization will be an open question. Technology has always carried human values but is not assumed to be neutral. As one of the hottest technological means at the moment, the Metaverse will have a great impact on the video media and the media industry, with both opportunities and challenges. The discussion of substantive issues should be people-oriented. The core value of intelligence is that people's morality, personality, soul, spirit, memory, etc. are different from the spiritual activities of other objects and creatures. The original intention of developing the Metaverse is to return to the open structure of the Internet through the adoption of virtual reality integration technology in human society, so that the next generation Internet can truly realize the essence of decentralization, interconnection, trust and collaboration.

As the Metaverse integrates and transcends a range of previous new Internet media information technologies, it compensates for the lack of media elements and levels of fine-grained granularity. Its historical characteristics of "deep media" have a close and complex internal connection with human beings, history, and the real world, and become the "media of all media" in human social activities, strengthening the "communication of communication" (ie "meta-communication"), is reshaping future media evolution at the macro level. Since the metaverse is only one possible future social and media form, some scholars have also attempted to elucidate the meta using the methods of media archaeology and the conceptual history of parody and parody of Frederick Frederick Jameson. The concept of the universe and its transcendental properties of media space-time. Some scholars have pondered the value, crisis and future of Internet platforms during the "hypercosmic turn" period. They believe that the hypercosmic turn will disrupt the current global Internet platform landscape, but platforms will also continue to challenge digital governance with the help of "hypercosmic capitalism".

5.3   The Monopoly and Supervision Mechanism of Metaverse Short Videos

The Metaverse will develop into a platform-like or a virtual world that is inclusive, and in this case, the problem of monopoly will be avoided. The Metaverse ultimately relies on a combination of technology, resources, labor and other factors, so there must be some capital in it. It can be said that the Metaverse is a model that needs to rely on strong financial power to operate. It needs a method with its own internal circulation, so that each industrial chain, ecological chain and each industrial chain can be operated, handed over and connected to each other. Helping to provide resources for mutual use can promote the deeper and far-reaching development of the Metaverse. As for the dissemination of Metaverse short videos, if there is a monopoly problem, then its coverage area is relatively wide, which will have a series of the weakening effects on the operation of the overall economic operation and industrial chain, which will cause some industries to operate actively. While other industries were forced to transform or disappear. At the same time, the metaverse must be the carrier of big data, so the dissemination of short videos must have a series of data flowing in the metaverse. If these data are forced to be monopolized, it will bring a series of irresistible consequences.

At the same time, the rapid expansion of short videos is inseparable from the algorithmic recommendation mechanism based on user portraits. Behind the big data algorithm is a collection of sophisticated user portrait databases, which can be roughly divided into basic portraits and advanced portraits. Basic portraits include basic personal information such as the user's gender, age, region, occupation, and income. Advanced portraits are based on dynamic analysis, data, statistics and documentation of user interaction behavior, including users' value preferences, consumption habits, emotional tendencies, etc. At present, the supervision and governance of short video platforms, mainly focus on issues such as film and television copyright disputes and excessive vulgarity of content (Jung and Choi, 2022). There are still large loopholes in the authenticity of massive short video content, information, the correctness of value orientation, and the control of the quality of products recommended by the platform.

5.4 Thoughts and Values of Metaverse Short Video Media Dissemination of Content

At present, the dissemination of short video media has gone through a certain stage of development, so some people become popular overnight, which is the content of entrepreneurship, and some follow the trend to carry out online publicity or become Internet celebrity anchors, then this also accelerates the yuan development of the universe. In the process of accelerating and rapidly promoting the dissemination of short video media, we must begin to reflect on the dissemination content of short videos. Each author has a different worldview, ideology and values of the metaverse, and video creation is homogeneous. The phenomenon is very serious now, blindly pursuing traffic and click-through rates, gaining attention and creating topical heat, and gradually forming a fixed production line in the process of nurturing products, including but not limited to re-engraving topics, imitating people, content editing, editing The soundtrack has highly similar behaviors, and even some short video products have poor ideological values, poor public opinion orientation, and spread false, outdated, and even pornographic and violent information. For example, the recent outbreak of teenagers was injured due to imitating short videos, family relationships broke down due to indulging in rewarding short video anchors, and people's property losses caused by false fund-raising news misleading. This limits the development space of the short video media metaverse. In recent years, the rapid iteration of emerging media technologies has led to the emergence of a large number of industry bubbles, and expectations of technological development can easily fall into the "progressive myth" criticized by Vincent Mosco (2009). Only by breaking the blind worship of technology can we find effective commercial landing scenarios for emerging media technologies. Just as the once-popular podcasts have stagnated in recent years, the era of "getting listeners as long as they are" is over, posing new challenges for podcasting sustainability (Deutsch, 2021). In the future, the podcast industry will experience a stage of shuffling and precipitation after rapid development. Practitioners must seriously reflect on what content means to their audiences, rebuild their own industry development rules, and ensure that the podcasting industry can maintain high-quality sustainable development (Nuzum, 2021). After a short burst of growth, podcasting has entered the track of healthy development of the bubble. Today's podcast may be tomorrow's metaverse. For the continuous development of media technology, while paying close attention to its development potential, it is also necessary to prudently judge possible industry bubbles and be alert to the "shining thing syndrome" in media technological change, so as to promote technological change to better serve the world Development of the news media industry.

6 Summary

In short, the metaverse has a bright future. It will break the boundaries between virtual and reality, online and offline, expand its boundaries infinitely, maintain the trend of sustainable development, surpass and break through the limitations of the previous generation of mobile Internet, and form a new "chaotic" universe. However, the construction of the Metaverse requires a long process. The complex effect of the integration of various technologies and industries in the Metaverse is also a huge ecological space created, shared and coexisted by the public, companies, governments and organizations, with huge impacts and change. Zuckerberg said the Metaverse is a vision that spans many companies and entire industries. One of the main scenarios for the application of the Metaverse in short video media communication should form an effective symbiotic interaction mechanism with the Metaverse. On the one hand, Metaverse technology helps media communication, and the transformation and upgrading of the industry; on the other hand, short video media and the industry are Metaverse The creation of Metaverse constantly replenishes energy, becoming an important new territory for the application of the Metaverse, leading the future dissemination.

Acknowledgements. This research was supported by Research on the Influence Path and Action Mechanism of Enterprise Financialization on the Balanced Development of the Real Economy under the Background of Economic Uncertainty(No. SZIIT2022SK009); Research on the High Quality Development of Shenzhen Industrial System Under the New Development Pattern of Double Cycle (No. SZIIT2021SK010).

References

Jung, W.-J., Choi, N.: A study on the advancement of makerspace as a digital transformation platform (2022)

Mosco, V.: Working-class network society: communication technology and the information have-less in urban china. J. Am. Soc. Inform. Sci. Technol. **60**(13), 2593–2595 (2009)

Latour, B.: Reassembling the Social: An Introduction to Actor-Network-Theory, pp. 171–172. Oxford University Press, New York (2005)

Van Dijck, J., Poell, T., de Waal, M.: The Platform Society: Public Values in a Connective World, p. 138. Oxford University Press, New York (2018)

"Introducing Meta," Youtube, https://www.youtube.com/watch?v=pjNI9K1D_xo, 20220209 visit

Shaw, X.: Microsoft Cloud at Lgnite 2021: Metaverse, AI and Hyperconnectivity in a Hybrid World, Microsoft, https://blogs.microsoft.com/blog/2021/11/02/microsoft-cloud-at-ignite-2021-metaverse-ai-and-hyperconnectivity-in-a-hybrid-world, 20211102 visit

"Metaverse May Be $ 800 Billion Market, Next Tech Platform," Bloomberg, https://www.bloomberg.com/professional/blog/meta-verse-may-be-800-billion-market-next-tech-platform/, 20220306 visit

The Exploration on Ethical Problems
of Educational Metaverse

Yi Li[✉], Wei Wei, and Jinhong Xu

Shenzhen Institute of Information Technology, Shenzhen Guangdong
518172, People's Republic of China
liyiify@126.com

Abstract. In recent years, the Metaverse is gaining traction. It is playing an increasingly important role in our lives. The year of 2021 is referred to the first year of the Metaverse. Researches all over the world on the Metaverse showed an explosive force beyond imagination. Beginning with the concept of the Metaverse and the application in educational Metaverse as the guidance, this paper discusses the ethical issues of educational Metaverse based on background of the Metaverse. Ultimately the biggest problem of the Metaverse is a human beings problem. That is to realize the purpose of people-oriented education. This paper mainly examines ethical problems of Metaverse from two aspects. Firstly, the problem of individual autonomy in the educational Metaverse is clearly specified. Secondly, we investigate the issues of privacy in the educational Metaverse. In addition, a series of minor problems such as data distortion, technical training and challenges for teachers are also discussed in detail.

Keywords: Metaverse · Educational metaverse · Ethical issue · Individual autonomy problem · Privacy problem

1 Introduction

Since the outbreak of COVID-19 worldwide in 2020, people's travel in the real world is often restricted. More and more people move their lives and work to the Internet, such as telecommuting, online teaching and online conference, and so forth, which objectively accelerate the application and popularization of information technology. A large number of people need to spend more time online and in virtual spaces, and spend much more time in digital world. The impact on the traditional education mode of the outbreak of COVID-19 is enormous. In order to ensure the continuity and stability of the education, many countries and regions in the world have to accept online-to-offline teaching model. And this model advances rapidly. China, in particular, has made outstanding achievements in this regard. Online-to-offline study model has become a habitual learning style for contemporary Chinese students. Before the outbreak of COVID-19, there is already involved some blended teaching model in China, but its popularity is far from excellent. They are Blended Teaching Method and Flipped Class Model or Flipped classroom. The former has already combined the online teaching and offline teaching time and space and

© The Author(s), under exclusive license to Springer Nature Switzerland AG 2022
L.-J, Zhang (Ed.): METAVERSE 2022, LNCS 13737, pp. 29–38, 2022.
https://doi.org/10.1007/978-3-031-23518-4_3

its affiliated teaching resources as a whole, they are teaching resources, teaching means, teaching methods and teaching ideas [1]. And the latter refers to inverting the traditional learning process, let learners get targeted knowledge and the concept in extracurricular by autonomous learning, classrooms became a place for interaction between teachers and students, which are mainly used to answer doubts, do reports and discussions to achieve better teaching results [2].

According to the Metaverse Development Report 2020–2021 [3] released by the New Media Research Center of Tsinghua University, 2020 is the tipping point for the virtualization of human society. There are three reasons. Firstly, under the quarantine policy of COVID-19, the online time of the whole society has increased significantly, and the Otaku Economy has developed rapidly. As a result, the epidemic has accelerated social virtualization. Secondly, online life has changed from a short-term exception state to a normal state, from a supplement of real world to a parallel world with the real world; Thirdly, with the opening of online and offline, human real life has begun to migrate to the virtual world on a large scale, and human beings have become a real and digital 'amphibious species'. This sets the stage for 2021 to be the first year of the Metaverse. Economist Jiaming Zhu believed that 2021 could be called the first year of the Metaverse. The explosion of the Metaverse is beyond imagination. Behind it is the critical mass effect of related elements of the Metaverse, which is similar to the Critical Mass experienced by the Internet in 1995 [4]. The rapid development of the Metaverse in the Internet will also cause changes in the educational model.

In January 2020, the World Economic Forum published the Schools of the Future Defining New Models of Education for the Fourth Industrial Revolution. In the context of the Fourth Industrial Revolution, Education 4.0: A Global Framework for Shifting Learning Content and Experiences Towards the Future has been put forward. In the report, it is redefining quality learning, calling for a critical shift in learning content and experience in global education, and proposing key approaches to innovative learning. It was mentioned in the report that Innova Schools in Peru has achieved very effective results by taking a multi-stakeholder approach to a collaborative blended -learning model.

Since the 18th National Congress of the Communist Party of China, The Party Central Committee centered by Xi Jinping attaches great importance to the education of contemporary college students. The report of the 19th National Congress of the Communist Party of China pointed out that 'a country prospers when its youth flourish, and a country becomes stronger when its youth flourish. When the young generation is idealistic, capable and responsible, the country will have a future and the nation will have hope.' It is difficult to stimulate the interest of students if they are lectured from the script, and it is more difficult to achieve the effect of entering the ear, into the brain and into the heart. Only innovation, the classroom can live, and then fire up. Xi Jinping attaches importance to the development of vocational education in China. In the new journey of building a modern socialist country in an all-round way, vocational education has a broad future and great potential [5]. Vocational education is closely linked to economic and social development, and it is of great significance to promoting employment and entrepreneurship, boosting economic and social development, and improving people's well-being. China actively promotes the high-quality development of vocational education and supports exchanges and cooperation in vocational education with other countries. China is ready to work with other countries to enhance mutual learning, joint contribution and shared benefits, jointly implement global development initiatives, and contribute to accelerating the implementation of the UN 2030 Agenda for Sustainable Development [6]. How to improve the teaching quality of education and to enhance the ideological and political literacy of college students has become a hot topic among scholars at present. Therefore, beginning with the concept of the Metaverse and the application in educational Metaverse as the guidance, this paper discusses the ethical issues of educational Metaverse based on background of the Metaverse. Ultimately the biggest problem of the Metaverse is a people problem. That is to realize the purpose of people-oriented education. This paper mainly examines ethical problems of Metaverse from two aspects. Firstly, the problem of individual autonomy in the educational Metaverse is clearly specified. Secondly, we investigate the issues of privacy in the educational Metaverse. In addition, a series of minor problems such as data distortion, technical training and challenges for teachers are also discussed in detail.

The remainder of this article is organized as follows. We give an introduction of related works in the Metaverse. In Sect. 3, the applications of the Metaverse in education is clearly described in detail. For Sect. 4, we discuss the ethical issues of educational Metaverse. Finally, the conclusions are summarized in Sect. 5.

2 Related Works

After the concept of the Metaverse became popular all over the world in 2021, the research on the Metaverse combined teaching in China and other countries increased year by year. The Metaverse is a kind of a mirror virtual world under the development of digital twin technology that integrates Augmented Reality (AR) based on virtual information of physical reality to supplement the information of real environment, Virtual Reality (VR) which presents virtual elements in virtual environment to simulate a kind of realistic reality and Mixed Reality (MR) which is a new visual environment produced by superimposing physical space and virtual space.

The term Metaverse first appeared in the book Avalanche by the famous science fiction writer Neil Stephenson in 1992. In this book, Neil Stephenson painted a picture of the hitherto futuristic Metaverse. 'Hiro is approaching the Street. It is the Broadway, the Champs Elysees of the Metaverse. It is the brilliantly lit boulevard that can be seen, miniaturized and backward, reflected in the lenses of his goggles. It does not really exist. But right now, millions of people are walking up and down it.' [7] In this virtual digital world that parallels to the real world, people in the real world have a virtual avatar in the Metaverse, and people use this virtual avatar to communicate and live.

It has been 20 years since the concept of the Metaverse appeared. However, people around the world have very different understandings of the Metaverse, and there is no recognized authoritative definition. Matthew Ball [8] offers a widely accepted definition in his article. The Metaverse is a massively scaled and interoperable network of real-time rendered 3D virtual worlds which can be experienced synchronously and persistently by an effectively unlimited number of users with an individual sense of presence, and with continuity of data, such as identity, history, entitlements, objects, communications, and payments. Ashutosh Gupta [9] considers that the Metaverse is a collective virtual space, created by the convergence of virtually enhanced physical and digital reality. In other words, it is device-independent and is not owned by a single vendor. It is an independent virtual economy, enabled by digital currencies and nonfungible tokens (NFTs). A Metaverse represents a combinatorial innovation, as it requires multiple technologies and trends to function. Contributing tech capabilities include AR, flexible work styles, head-mounted displays (HMDs), an AR cloud, the Internet of Things (IoT), 5G, artificial intelligence (AI) and spatial technologies.

In China, according to the definition of the 2021 research report [10] by Tianfeng Securities, the Metaverse aims to create a virtual digital second world independent of the real world, enabling users to live freely as digital identities. The core is sustainability, real-time, no access restrictions (multiple terminals), economic function (having its own closed-loop economy), connectivity (connecting the real world through terminals), and creativity (PGC&UGC).

A team from Tsinghua University in Shenyang gave a comprehensive definition in the Metaverse White Paper [11]. The Metaverse is to integrate a variety of new technologies and to produce a new type of virtuality and reality combination of Internet applications and social form, which is based on extended reality technology which is providing immersive experience, based on the number of twin technology which is generating a mirror image of the real world, based on block chain technology which is structuring economic system and integrating the virtual world and real world in the economic system, social system, identity system closely. And it allows each user to do content production and world editing. It also argues that the Metaverse is still an evolving synopsis, with various participants enriching the meaning of the Metaverse in their own ways.

3   The Application of the Metaverse in Education

The concept of the Metaverse seems very complex. As a new upgrade and future ecology of the Internet, it embodies all the imagination of people for the future work, life, entertainment and other spiritual life. The core of Metaverse infrastructure is virtual technology, which is a three-dimensional virtual space with three 'I' features simulated by computer. That is, the Metaverse has the feature of imagination, immersion and interaction [12]. The elaborately made simulated space enables users to get immersive experience. It also opens up myriad possibilities for the future development of the educational Metaverse.

In Europe countries, Second Life [19], an open and free virtual reality platform developed by Linden Laboratories, was launched in 2003 and became the first phenomenal virtual world. Sweden became the first country to open a virtual embassy in Second Life in May 2007. Teachers could build teaching scenes and carry out task-based teaching in Second Life. Second Life provides an open learning space for language learners to communicate freely, and some of the world's top universities, such as Harvard University, has built virtual campuses through Second Life to pave the way for related research. Roblox [20] has been trying to reach into the education space for a long time while running its gaming community. The focus has been on a child's programming curriculum around its own game development programs. Through this series of official tutorials,

Roblox is able to convert a large number of ordinary players into game developers for the platform each year. And it keep them producing games for the platform, and its working. Roblox is devoting more resources to education. By partnering with schools and educational institutions to provide teachers with free handouts and lessons, Roblox has spread its programming classes to elementary and middle schools in the U.S. and abroad. Many teachers use the Roblox curriculum to teach programming, and hundreds of training institutions offer specialized Roblox programming classes. In addition, Roblox runs summer coding camps that take students to high schools and colleges to immerse in programming while learning about interpersonal communication and teamwork. In 2021, Roblox invested 10 million dollars to develop three educational games for middle school student, high school students and college students. One will teach robotics, one will focus on space exploration, and one will help students to learn careers and concepts in disciplines like computer science, engineering and biomedicine. The three games, which do not offer virtual goods for sale, are available in schools on a non-profit basis. The move to bring educational video games to classrooms around the world is part of Roblox's strategy to expand its user base and build a Metaverse.

Meta's cash burn began in October 2021, when Zuckerberg announced at Facebook Connect 2021 that Facebook was officially rebranding itself as Meta, making an all-out bet on the Metaverse. Zuckerberg posted a virtual selfie to Meta on August 16, 2022 to celebrate the launch of Horizon Worlds, a Metaverse social platform, in France and Spain. He then updated the photos again on Meta and Instagram. In contrast to the old image, the avatar appears more natural and three-dimensional with layered hair, added highlights in the eyes and more realistic ears. In addition, a contrast of light and shadow was added to make the figure appear more realistic.

Virtual reality platforms such as Second Life, Roblox, and Meta (Facebook) break through the limitations of the physical classroom to provide a free learning space, which is expected to integrate into a Metaverse of education in the future.

The educational Metaverse is also thriving at home. The first National VR and Visualization Technology and Application Conference was held in November 2001, which was sponsored by VR and Visualization Technology Committee of Chinese Computer Society and hosted by Academy of Armored Force Engineering and Beihang University. In order to improve the teaching quality and promote the development of higher education, the Ministry of Education of China launched the construction of the national virtual simulation experimental teaching center in 2015. In order to implement the relevant deployment of the 14th Five-Year education development plan and to accelerate the construction of virtual teaching and research offices, the General Office of the Ministry of Education of China announced the first batch of 439 [13] virtual teaching and research office construction pilot list on February 15, 2022, and the second batch of 218 [14] virtual teaching and research office construction pilot list on May 19. A total of 657 pilot construction projects have been approved twice. Beihang University has been approved 10 virtual teaching and research sections, including 4 courses (group) teaching, 3 professional construction, 2 teaching and research reform topics and 1 virtual teaching and research section for the compilation principle course of 101 Plan. More and more schools begin to study virtual simulation technology. In 2019, the Ministry of Education of China certified 401 [15] national virtual simulation experimental teaching projects. On August 3rd, 2021, the Department of Vocational Education and Adult Education of the Ministry of Education of China determined 215 [16] vocational education demonstration virtual simulation training base cultivation projects. Among them, two schools in Shenzhen have been shortlisted as virtual simulation training bases, namely the intelligent ICT virtual simulation training base of Shenzhen Polytechnic and the 5G all-scene and all-business vocational education demonstration virtual simulation training base of Shenzhen Institute of Information Technology. Tencent, Bytedance, Baidu, NetEase and other companies are also actively engaged in virtual reality Metaverse business. With the development of science and technology and the promotion of policy, there are increasingly related researches in China and plenty of studies on the educational Metaverse.

4 The Ethical Issues of Educational Metaverse

At present, the Metaverse has not yet been formally born, but the ethical problems of the educational Metaverse can be seen by referring to the lessons of previous virtual worlds and the ethical problems presented by existing technologies such as big data and intelligent algorithms. Ultimately the biggest problem of the Metaverse is a human beings problem. That is how to achieve the purpose of people-oriented education.

Firstly, the problem of individual autonomy in the educational Metaverse is discussed. In January 2020, the World Economic Forum put forward the Global Framework for Education 4.0, which mentioned the suggestion of developing students' human-centered skills and moving towards a true learning-centered education. Global school systems are required to develop students' human-centric skills, those are cooperation, empathy, social awareness and global citizenship. Those skills can ensure that children take responsibility for shaping inclusive and equitable societies of the future. However, in the world of the educational Metaverse, human beings can use their imagination to build it. Anyone can have everything that they want in virtual world. In the educational Metaverse, education is no longer limited by time, place, identity and other restrictions. So will human beings transfer all education in the real society to the virtual society? Jeremy Bailenson's experiments [18] examined to what extent our avatars are extensions of ourselves. It showed that living in a virtual world also affects our offline behavior. In virtual interactions based on self-presentation, avatars can influence the users' perception, attitude and behavior, whether consciously or unconsciously, which is known as the Proteus effect in psychology. In a social setting, if something goes wrong with your avatar, it seems to trigger the same neural circuits as if something went wrong with the real you.

In terms of individuals following the social order, people will become increasingly domesticated in the Metaverse, while machines or virtual avatars will become more and more humanized, blurring the boundary between the virtual and the real. Are people subjects of the real world or the virtual world, or not subjects at all? Therefore, we should be alert to the humanistic crisis caused by the reversal of the relationship between man and technology [17].

On the social level, science and technology make people expect a fairer and more equal world, and make people expect more equal education. People used to think that the Internet would change the current state of education and ordinary people could also receive the guidance of famous teachers on the Internet. However, this is not the case. It is always restricted by different institutions, economies and cultures. So will things change in the Metaverse? Zuckerberg has emphasized for many times that in the Metaverse, the way of decentralized entitlements will be realized and more decentralization will be realized. However, the function of the Metaverse is mainly to calculate, maintain and regulate, record users' footprints, identify directions, determine time and space, and establish data indexes. It is more widely used in the structure of people's daily life and the organization of power. It shows how data supports our existence. Intelligent algorithms which are ubiquitous in the Metaverse have simplified autonomy, that is, action autonomy, while moral autonomy is ignored by designers. In the process of program design, a lot of correlation thinking is adopted while causal thinking is weakened in order to establish connections and to make decisions in the complex events by algorithms. And then do humans still have moral autonomy in the Metaverse? The Metaverse integrates VR, AR, MR, 5G, cloud computing and other technologies. It is a highly motivated and highly institutionalized mandatory system, and general users are completely incapable of understanding its operation, let alone changing it. This algorithmic bias is an important information ethical problem in the era of algorithmic information. It has a non-neutral influence on users in the process of information production, distribution and verification, resulting in the spread of one-sided and inaccurate information concepts. Although the algorithm program can exist independently of manual operation and recommend information to users from a relatively objective standpoint, the deep-rooted bias that may be hidden in it has been constantly exposed in practice. How to maintain the uniqueness of human beings and adhere to the people-oriented ethics is the first ethical problem in the Metaverse age.

Secondly, the issue of privacy in the education Metaverse is studied. The value of the Metaverse to schooling is reflected in the field of learning, teaching and education, where the Metaverse creates an immersive learning experience. It brings an immersive learning environment. In the existing online education or blended education combining online and offline, teachers and students generally respond that this method can improve students' learning interest, attention, enthusiasm and innovation, relieve anxiety in real class, improve communication skills, and ultimately improve students' learning quality. In the Metaverse, it is a way not only to enable the real world, but also transcend the virtual environment. It can transcend the existing online teaching means, so that students can learn freely and productively. Students can immerse themselves in the learning environment with the immersive nature of virtual reality technology. They can explore the simulation scene in the way of personal experience and feel the scene content from the first perspective. Virtual reality technology can also help to enrich students' imagination and to improve their creative ability. Digitalization is an advantage of the educational Metaverse, which can make education more diversified and learning more diversified. But at the same time, in the process of building the educational Metaverse, a lot of data mining and analysis, such as human beings, real environment, physical existence, etc. are obtained from real life. Moreover, the builders of the educational Metaverse are some enterprises. These companies are in the hands of some people. They will master countless private information in the process of building the educational Metaverse, as a result the ability to ensure the security of data is required. High and new technology will continue to be rapidly introduced and applied in school education. In the data collection of school environment and teaching links, AI technologies such as face recognition and voice recognition will be applied to provide comprehensive, convenient and visual quantitative indicators and management tools for educational managers at all levels to provide front-line teachers with data representations of students' learning behaviors, learning processes and learning outcomes, to provide personalized and adaptive learning guidance for each learner, and to achieve the goal of reducing burden, increasing efficiency, balancing quality education reform through the empowerment of educational technology. However, the special feature of the educational Metaverse is that in order to facilitate management, teachers and students also have to upload real information in the course of class, including the personal information of teachers, work units, students' personal information, courses learned, and so on. The data is taken from the real world. The educational Metaverse with artificial intelligence as its core technology completely depends on data for its decision-making ability, and data will bring privacy problems. How to ensure the security of these data is a big problem to be considered in the educational Metaverse.

Of course, the educational Metaverse will also face some other challenges, such as data distortion, technical training, teacher challenges, and so on. If the individual shapes the personal virtual image in educational Metaverse, considering to hidden identity, they fill in the data distortion, which leads to their images in the education Metaverse neither completely true personality of virtualization, nor of the will of individual real full expression. Most images are just partial reflection to people's real personality, sometimes even the opposite. This distorted data is bound to hamper the popularity of the education industry in the Metaverse. The educational Metaverse is the result of the integration and development of multiple technologies, which means that after the construction of the educational Metaverse, a large number of technical personnels are needed to provide technical training for ordinary teachers to improve their computer-aided instruction ability and information level, which takes a long time and costs a lot. Moreover, it increases the workload of teachers and puts forward higher requirements for teachers in the education Metaverse. The information technology of contemporary college students in China is extremely developed, and most of them can adapt to the changes brought by the educational Metaverse in a very short time. If the teachers cannot increase their knowledge reserve as soon as possible, the gap between teachers and students will be widened invisibly. This raises the panic of teachers' professionalism. Teachers not only have certain pressure in classroom design, but also have a large workload in after-class testing and evaluation. In the process of teaching, there may be strangers' trespass, spread violence, illegal information and other problems, which bring great difficulty to teachers' teaching management.

5 Conclusions

The ideal educational Metaverse is a utopia world of high freedom, high openness and high tolerance. It is a collection of various complex relations in real society. How to construct the ethical framework of the educational Metaverse in the decentralized framework still needs to be explored from multiple perspectives. As a surreal virtual space, it is necessary to mine and upload the identity attributes, physiological reactions and social relations of the participants of the educational Metaverse, which will inevitably involve the disclosure of personal information. How to manage and use these data and how to prevent crimes based on these data is a big challenge.

From the Internet to the mobile Internet and to the Metaverse, technology is developing rapidly. The deep integration of science and technology and education is the inevitable development direction of future education. The educational Metaverse created by the richness and integration of virtual reality platform can realize the normalization of teaching resources to share and to communicate. The educational Metaverse gives a new meaning to traditional education, and enriches traditional teaching from content to scene. However, virtual reality technology does not deny the traditional education model, nor can it replace the responsibility of teachers. Teachers act as guides and leaders in the integration of science and technology into teaching that should combine the development of technology, treat technology from a rational perspective, and promote the integration of industry-university-research teaching.

Acknowledgements. This research was supported by Research on the Practice of Online and Offline Blended Teaching (No. SZIIT2021SK035), Research on the High Quality Development of Shenzhen Industrial System Under the New Development Pattern of Double Cycle (No. SZIIT2021SK010) and Research on the Supply of Community Senior Citizen Education in Shenzhen under the Background of Aging (No. Ybzz20009).

References

1. Lu, L., Xu, X.: From 'Blended' to 'Chaos': a discussion on the future teaching model from the perspective of the metaverse – a case study of the curation course in cloud exhibition hall of east china normal university. Library Tribune **42**(01), 53–61 (2022)
2. Ma, X., Zhao, G., Wu, T.: An empirical study on flipped classroom teaching of college information technology public course. J. Dist. Educ. **31**(01), 79–85 (2013)
3. Tsinghua University, Metaverse Development Research Report 2020-2021, 2020: 9-9
4. Tsinghua University, Metaverse Development Research Report 2020-2021, 2020: 8-8
5. Vocational education has a great future http://www.moe.gov.cn/jyb_xwfb/s5148/202104/t20 210429_529103.html?authkey=boxdr3, last accessed 21 September 2022
6. Congratulations to World Congress for the Development of Vocational and Technical Education by Xi jinping, http://paper.people.com.cn/rmrb/html/2022-08/20/nw.D110000renmrb_2 0220820_1-01.htm, last accessed 21 September 2022
7. Neal Stephenson: Snow Crash. Penguin Press, p. 13 (2011)
8. Matthew, B.: Framework for the Metaverse, The Metaverse Primer (Jun 29 2021). https://www.matthewball.vc/all/forwardtotheMetaverseprimer?ref=hackernoon.com, last accessed 23 September 2022
9. Ashutosh Gupta: What Is a Metaverse?. https://www.gartner.com/en/articles/what-is-a-Met averse, last accessed 23 September 2022
10. Feng, C., Wen, H.: The Metaverse: Gaming's Ark to Virtual Reality. TF Securities (2021)
11. Tsinghua University: Metaverse Development Research Report 2020-2021, 2020: 14-14
12. Thomas, B.: Interaction, Imagination and Immersion Some Research Needs. In: Proceedings of the ACM Symposium on Virtual Reality Software and Technology (VRST '00). Association for Computing Machinery, pp.1–7. New York, NY, USA (2000)

13. The First Batch of Virtual Teaching and Research Office Construction Pilot of The Ministry of Education of China, http://www.moe.gov.cn/srcsite/A08/s7056/202203/t20220322_609822.html, last accessed 21 September 2022
14. The Second Batch of Virtual Teaching and Research Office Construction Pilot of the Ministry of Education of China, http://www.moe.gov.cn/srcsite/A08/s7056/202206/t20220602_634144.html, last accessed 21 September 2022
15. The Ministry of Education of China, http://www.moe.gov.cn/, last accessed 21 September 2022
16. Virtual Simulation Training Base Training Project in China, http://www.moe.gov.cn/s78/A07/A07_sjhj/202108/t20210804_548809.html, last accessed 21 September 2022
17. Li, L.: Algorithmic Humanism: A Philosophical Outline of Information Values in the Intelligent Age. Xinhua Publishing House, Beijing (2021)
18. Yee, N., Bailenson, J.: The proteus effect: the effect of transformed self-representation on behavior. Hum. Commun. Res. **33**, 271–290 (2007). https://doi.org/10.1111/j.1468-2958.2007.00299.x
19. The Second Life: https://secondlife.com/, last accessed 21 September 2022
20. Roblox: https://roblox.qq.com/, last accessed 21 September 2022

Application and Industry Track

Research on the Application and Risk Prevention of Metaverse in Vocational Education

Xuan Li[✉]

ShenZhen Institute of Information Technology, ShenZhen 518172, People's Republic of China
lee7909@163.com

Abstract. The Metaverse is a new concept born with the rapid development of information technology. The state has begun to lay out the applications of the Metaverse in various fields. Education is the main application scenario and innovation channel of the Metaverse. The features of the Metaverse, such as immersion, constructiveness, interactivity, decentralization and openness, are highly compatible with the future educational form. The era of Metaverse needs vocational schools to cognize the Metaverse objectively and make use of the Metaverse technology to empower vocational education, to promote the reform of teaching methods in vocational education, and to solve the difficulties in vocational education. At the same time, we should calmly analyze the possible challenges of privacy risk, ethical risk, addiction risk, and consider the effective measures to prevent the risk from occurring, with a view to providing some reference and inspiration for the high-quality development of the vocational education.

Keywords: Metaverse · Vocational education · Application and risk prevention

1 Introduction

The year 2021 is called the first year of the Metaverse, with the renaming of Facebook as Meta, the world's largest social media site, the capital investment and development potential of many domestic and foreign companies in the Metaverse have been activated. The Metaverse will not only completely change the mode of human social communication, life and work, but also completely change the mode of human learning, which has aroused heated discussion in the field of education. The outbreak and spread of Covid-19 has accelerated technological change in education and restarted large-scale online education across the country, with far-reaching and more sophisticated online learning models developing significantly faster in the face of adversity, the integration of technology and education is getting closer and closer, but the problems such as insufficient interaction, insufficient contextualization and poor learning experience have not been effectively solved. The educational field is one of the core application scenarios of the Metaverse, and the integration of the Metaverse and education will bring profound changes to the existing educational work.

As one of the types of education, the vocational education universe of education will give new impetus and direction to its development. Therefore, this paper analyzes the

© The Author(s), under exclusive license to Springer Nature Switzerland AG 2022
L.-J. Zhang (Ed.): METAVERSE 2022, LNCS 13737, pp. 41–54, 2022.
https://doi.org/10.1007/978-3-031-23518-4_4

connotation and characteristics of the Metaverse and the education Metaverse, explores the application prospect of the Metaverse in the field of vocational education, and analyzes the possible risks and challenges that the Metaverse may bring to vocational education, with the aim of providing reference for the reform and innovative development of vocational education in the future.

2 The Metaverse and the Educational Metaverse

2.1 The Connotation of the Metaverse

The concept of the Metaverse is in a process of rapid growth and evolution. Different scholars have defined the Metaverse from the perspectives of technology and philosophy, and there is no unified conclusion yet. The Shenyang team of Tsinghua University defines the Metaverse as a new type of Internet application and social form that integrates a variety of new technologies. Zhang Xiaheng et al. believe that Metaverse is an Internet field based on the interaction of virtual reality world constructed by information technology, Internet technology and digital technology. Liu Geping believes that the Metaverse represents the latest stage of the development of visual immersion technology. Its essence is an online digital space parallel to the real world, and it is becoming a practical field for the innovation and development of human society. Some researchers believe that Metaverse is based on technologies such as digital twins, artificial intelligence, human-computer interaction, Internet of Things, and high-speed communication. It is created to meet people's needs for deep immersion, cross-domain social entertainment, and surreal creation. An ecological civilization space that is parallel to the real world and independent of the integration of the real world and society.

Regardless of the current interpretation of the perspective of the Metaverse, that the Metaverse is after the PC Internet and mobile internet after the new generation of the Internet has become a common understanding. The Metaverse is an important part of the digital economy era and the next stage of the Internet. It consists of augmented reality (AR), virtual reality (VR), mixed reality (MR), immersive vision, blockchain, cloud computing, Digital Twins, artificial intelligence, big data, 3D and other technologies to support the virtual reality world, is driving the entire world from the industrial era to the digital economy era upgrade.

2.2 The Properties of the Educational Metaverse

Metaverse provides a new breakthrough educational environment and tools for education, which can provide teachers and learners with an immersive interactive field of teaching, to meet the teaching and learning needs of teachers and students in the physical world and virtual world. The integration of the Metaverse and the field of education is bound to contain infinite possibilities for development. The educational Metaverse is a kind of Metaverse, which is based on the concept of Metaverse and oriented to the field of education, and can be regarded as the application of the Metaverse in the field of education, it is the deep fusion of education and the Metaverse. The teaching subject is endowed with digital identity by the virtual world constructed by the Metaverse to carry out educational activities. The educational Metaverse is not a simple copy of the teaching situation in the real world, nor is it a pile of technical means in the field of education, but a new form of education.

Industrial transformation has led to changes in the demand for talents. In order to cultivate and meet the employment needs of the development of the digital economy, the government has issued a number of policies to promote the digital transformation of education, and also play a role in promoting the development of the education Metaverse. In 2015, the government work report put forward the concept of Internet+, and implemented the Internet+ action plan in July to develop Internet+ education. In 2020, the State Council issued the National Vocational Education Reform Implementation Plan (20 Vocational Education) and proposed to build a new system of Internet+ Vocational Education, innovate a new model of Internet+ Vocational Education, explore new rules of Internet+ Vocational Education, Cultivate a new mechanism of Internet+ Vocational Education to meet the requirements of industrial upgrading. In 2021, the government work report proposes to accelerate the construction of new infrastructure. In July, six major departments including the Ministry of Education issued guidelines on promoting the construction of new infrastructure for education and a high-quality education support system. In January 2022, the key points of the Ministry of Education's work were also put forward to implement the strategic action of education digitalization.

From the perspective of application scope, the Metaverse of education has the characteristics of virtual and reality interweaving, human and machine cooperation, and school and society connection. The Metaverse of education integrates the realistic elements of educational content, educational aim, role relationship and management mode into its logical system, and generates a new educational system based on the related characteristics of virtual space and educational system, so that teachers and students can construct multi-channel interaction with virtual identity, and use terminal equipment to simulate audio-visual interaction and other interactive effects, to complete learning interaction and communication. As a technological ecosystem linking virtual and reality, the educational Metaverse makes the labor relationship between educational subject and technology become close, intelligent technology provides differentiated teaching design for educational subjects through accurate learner portraits, and realizes more flexible and efficient cooperative mechanism between human and machine. The Metaverse of education promotes the transformation and development of knowledge and ability by connecting virtual space with real space, connecting school system with social system, dispelling the Wall and boundary between education and society.

From the perspective of the technical framework, the education Metaverse requires high-speed data transmission technology and strong computer processing capabilities, and requires the support of core technologies such as network communication technology, computing technology, Internet of Things technology, artificial intelligence technology, interactive technology, and blockchain technology. Network communication technology. Education Metaverse needs a smooth network environment to support the normal operation of large-scale virtual mirror learning scenarios. 5G network technology can meet the transmission requirements of Metaverse's massive data and ensure the operation of virtual learning scenarios. Computing technology. The application scenarios of the education cloud universe have high requirements on the performance of the client and the carrying capacity of the equipment, such as 3D graphics rendering in educational applications. Cloud computing technology transfers the data processing work in the Metaverse to the data center for processing. After processing, it is transmitted to the user side, which can solve the problem of insufficient computing power on the user side and provide a solid hardware environment foundation for teaching scenarios. Internet of Things technology. Use information sensors to connect devices in the real world with the network according to specific communication protocols, providing a transmission channel for the education Metaverse to perceive signals from the physical world and access the education Metaverse. Artificial intelligence technology. Thanks to the rapid development of current artificial intelligence technology, intelligent tutors, intelligent assessment, intelligent decision-making, etc. have been widely developed and application. Interaction technology. Through the integration of visual interaction technologies such as virtual reality (VR) and augmented reality (AR), it brings teachers and students immersion and flow state of seamless transition between the virtual world and the real world, providing a deep immersion experience and an immersive interactive experience. Blockchain technology. The decentralization, distribution, traceability, high trust and other technical features of this technology ensure the integrity and security of the data and information generated in the process of education management and teaching, which can be used for the certification of learning outcomes, credit bank construction, digital resource management and distribution, ecological construction of open educational resources, self-organized operation of digital campus communities, etc., provide knowledge sharing and certification guarantees based on rules and algorithm operations (Fig. 1).

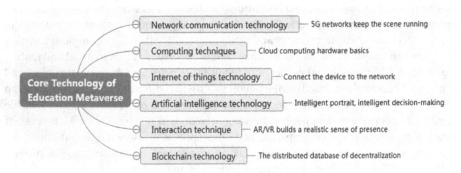

Fig. 1. Schematic diagram of the main core technologies of the education Metaverse

3   The Application Prospect of Metaverse in Vocational Education

Vocational education, as one of the types of education in my country, cultivates high-quality modern talents with professional theoretical knowledge and practical operation ability. Today, the elements of vocational education are undergoing profound changes. Artificial intelligence, online and offline hybrid teaching, and virtual simulation technology have achieved good development in the field of vocational education. Information technology empowers vocational school teaching and vocational training. It has become a kind of The new normal. However, the current vocational education still has problems such as insufficient teachers, weak learning motivation, and loose structure of production and education, which impede the improvement of the quality of vocational education. The education Metaverse provides new ways, means that many new possibilities for vocational education, which is expected to promote the high-quality development of vocational education. However, the specific impact path and degree of influence of the education Metaverse on vocational education remains to be explored. This paper analyzes the current predicament in the development of vocational education, and then starts from the core technologies of the education Metaverse to explore the specific applications of these technologies in vocational education, and how the occurrence of these applications will affect the ecology of vocational education.

3.1 The Main Difficulties in Vocational Education Development

Affected by the COVID-19, vocational colleges have effectively alleviated the problem of separation of time and space in teaching through online teaching, and maintained the normal teaching work of vocational schools in order to realize suspended classes without teaching, and without stopping learning. VR/AR technology has also begun to play a role in the field of vocational education. Seoul National University Hospital in South Korea used VR/AR technology to share real-time surgery at the 29th online academic conference of the Asian Society of Cardiovascular and Thoracic Surgery. However, some research studies have pointed out that when the characteristics of the given matching samples are consistent, the learning effect of online students is unsatisfactory, and most experimental courses and practical training courses are postponed until after returning to school, which affects the teaching goal of integrating theory and practice. In addition to these new problems, there are still low social recognition in the field of vocational education, imperfect vocational education system design, school-enterprise cooperation mere formality, mismatch between enterprise demand and talent supply, uneven teacher level, and lack of students' motivation to learn, the lack of professional experience and other problems and predicaments restrict the high-level development of vocational education.

3.1.1 The Social Recognition of Vocational Education is Low, and the Design of Vocational Education System is not Perfect

Students' access to higher education is blocked. Before the 1990s, technical secondary schools and junior colleges were favored by people, but after the expansion of higher education, these degrees lost their original aura. According to the 2020 data from the National Statistical Bulletin on the Development of Education, there were 182 fewer secondary vocational schools than the previous year. The number of students enrolled in vocational colleges has dropped year by year from 2010, and it has not recovered until 2019. Compared with 2010, the number of students in secondary vocational schools in 2020 has dropped by about 26%. Moreover, due to the imperfect design of the vocational education system, there is a lack of opportunities for vocational talents to adjust and choose, and there are insurmountable barriers between applied universities and comprehensive universities, and it is difficult to meet the needs of vocational talents to increase their studies (Fig. 2).

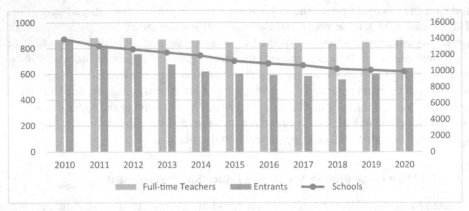

Fig. 2. Changes in the development trend of secondary vocational schools from 2010 to 2020 (unit: 10,000 people, 1000 school). Data source: Based on statistics from the Ministry of Education

3.1.2 School-Enterprise Cooperation is a Mere Formality, and There is a Mismatch Between Enterprise Demand and Talent Supply

In the past, vocational education provided solely by schools was out of touch with the actual needs of society. In addition to the outdated curriculum content, which was difficult to update in time with industrial progress, the teaching content was often a generic version, which was difficult to connect with the refined needs of enterprises. Therefore, many graduates of vocational colleges cannot get good job opportunities due to insufficient skill training, and enterprises are in short supply because they cannot recruit suitable skilled talents. Taking the automotive industry as an example, the current automotive majors are generally EFI electronic control and new energy intelligence, but some schools are still evaluating carburetor models. Vocational education is also trying to solve such problems by strengthening school-enterprise cooperation. However, due to the high mobility of technical personnel, enterprises cannot see a favorable input-output ratio and are unwilling to really invest in the long-term school-enterprise co-education process. It makes school-enterprise cooperation a mere formality and fails to really play an effective role.

3.1.3 There Are Differences in the Construction of Teaching Staff

In recent years, although my country has made certain achievements in the construction of vocational education teachers, there are still many deficiencies: Affected by factors such as natural geographical conditions, policies and regional economic levels, the teachers in underdeveloped areas are relatively small, and information The ability to apply technology needs to be strengthened. More teachers directly graduated from school to teach in vocational schools. They have insufficient experience in social practice and lack of knowledge updating ability. They need to be improved in terms of professional knowledge, teaching ability and comprehensive quality.

3.1.4 Students Lack Motivation in Learning and Lack of Professional Experience

Due to the weak learning foundation of most students in my country's vocational education and the poor subjective ability of learning, most of them are forced to be diverted. In the traditional classroom teaching method, the teacher is the lecturer of the classroom teaching, and the students accept and learn in a fixed manner, becoming a machine that passively accepts knowledge, and the learning process is quite boring. If students do not stimulate the subjective ability of learning, they will gradually lose their enthusiasm and self-confidence in learning. Moreover, before choosing a major, during the learning process, students in vocational colleges have few opportunities for career exploration and do not understand the real professional working environment, making it difficult to meet the changing development needs of enterprises after leaving the campus, or It is difficult to accept the reality of the working environment, thus giving up the major and engaging in work that does not correspond to the major.

3.2 The Application of Education Metaverse in Vocational Education

Applying new technologies to vocational education must be the only way for the development of the times. Education Metaverse technology enhances the interaction, immersion and sense of acquisition of the learning process of vocational education through scene empowerment, and provides a cheaper and more realistic skills training platform, breaking the online classroom of vocational education brought by two-dimensional network technology. Development bottleneck.

3.2.1 Application Scenarios of Education Metaverse Empowering Vocational Education

Artificial intelligence technology, Digital intelligent teachers provide personalized and innovative education. Teachers play a vital role in education and teaching, but from the reality of our country's current vocational colleges, there is still a shortage of high-quality double-qualified teachers. Using Metaverse, artificial intelligence and other technologies to create digital intelligent teachers can solve the problem of lack of teachers to a certain extent. Create digital intelligent teachers for specific majors and specific courses in vocational colleges, provide students with educational services at any time, answer students' questions, and provide personalized education for each student, which will alleviate the shortage of teachers in vocational colleges to a certain extent.so that students can feel the care and education of teachers at any time, so that education is always present and ubiquitous.

AR/VR interactive technology,create an immersive interactive teaching environment. In the field of education, immersion and interactivity are the most prominent advantages of VR technology. Based on VR/AR-based visual immersion technology, the virtual-real interface for learning the Metaverse becomes the access point for learning the Metaverse.Using human-machine interface equipment, network, cloud computing and other technologies, develop a targeted teaching environment for vocational education courses based on the Metaverse, and map the teaching content knowledge of high-level teachers, so that teachers and students can learn in a surreal environment. Immersive interactive teaching, as described in movies such as The Matrix and Ready Player One, teachers and students can learn, live and make friends in a virtual digital world by wearing human-machine interface devices, reshaping education and learning environment to promote deep learning and cognitive development of learners.

Virtual teaching equipment, reduce the cost of vocational education skills practice. Vocational colleges need to purchase and equip corresponding teaching equipment to train qualified industrial workers. However, teaching equipment is often expensive. Fiscal and taxation simulation platforms, industrial automation process platforms, etc. often require millions of funds. The school's site environment is very demanding, and some equipment upgrades and changes quickly, which puts forward higher requirements for vocational colleges. The lack of vocational skills practice environment is an important practical dilemma faced by vocational colleges, especially in underdeveloped areas and vocational colleges with tight funding. AR/VR can simulate expensive teaching equipment, and at the same time restore 100% mechanical equipment, it can also assist teachers in teaching, which greatly saves education costs. In vocational education, digital virtual teaching equipment is widely used to carry out practical training operations, which has broad market prospects and practical value in my country. At present, in aerospace, military and other fields, high-simulation digital virtual equipment is widely used in training; in general civilian industries, the fidelity, popularization and professionalism of digital virtual equipment need to be improved.

Blockchain technology, Promote the construction, sharing and sharing of digital resources featuring vocational education. The platform is the basic carrier of information-based education and teaching services. In recent years, certain achievements have been made in the construction of information-based platforms. For example, in March 2022, the National Smart Education Cloud Platform was officially launched. High-quality resources in the field have built an open and shared platform service model. However, there are still problems such as the inability of interconnection between various educational platforms at all levels, inconsistent platform data standards, ineffective data aggregation, and repeated platform construction. Vocational college teachers can only choose some different information platforms for teaching, which is not conducive to the accumulation and sharing of resources. The technological development trend of Metaverse provides a starting point for solving such problems. Using application technologies represented by blockchain to formulate compatible standards and protocols can promote the interconnection between open source platforms and platforms, and help cross-regional and cross-platform, data flow and aggregation. In addition, the technical features of blockchain technology such as decentralization and traceability ensure the integrity and security of data and information generated in the process of education management and teaching, which can be used for learning achievement certification, credit bank construction, and digital resource management, and distribution, ecological construction of open educational resources, etc. to provide certification guarantees.

3.2.2   The Impact of Education Metaverse on Vocational Education Ecology

The application of the core technologies of Education Metaverse in vocational education can not only bring enhanced effects to vocational education, but also help solve the difficulties of vocational education and shape a new vocational education ecology. No matter how technology develops, the essence of vocational education cannot be forgotten, and how to develop vocational education itself is something we need to think deeply about and make decisions.

Solve the problems of high cost, high risk and difficult implementation in vocational education. The education Metaverse is the product of digital development to a high level, and it is essentially digital software. Students enter the education Metaverse through AR/VR equipment, and carry out practical training such as human anatomy, surgical simulation, chemical experiment skills, mechanical operation, etc., which can greatly reduce teaching costs, and can also avoid dangerous accidents in the process of practical operation. Protect the lives and property of teachers and students. Education Metaverse uses technologies such as extended reality and digital twin to construct learning scenes, training scenes, and work scenes in virtual space, providing a highly realistic practical environment for teachers to carry out teaching activities. Participate in virtual practice, cultivate students' practical ability and operational skills, and solve difficult and difficult problems.

Promote the sharing of educational resources and solve the problem of unbalanced distribution of educational resources. In the educational form of industrial society and agricultural society, knowledge is monopolized. In the Metaverse era, educational elements are concentrated on the network platform, and the implementation of education will be based on individual choices to achieve educational equity. Education Metaverse uses digital technology to build digital teaching places, break through the shackles of geographical, economic, cultural and other factors on the teaching of vocational education, reduce the impact of external emergencies on educational activities, and enable students in underdeveloped areas with insufficient teachers. You can share high-quality vocational education teaching content, understand cutting-edge vocational education theory and career dynamics, and learn to use advanced industrial equipment. Through the mutually beneficial sharing of educational resources, the fairness of vocational education will be improved, and the regional differences in the quality of vocational education will be improved.

Realize the teaching of multi-scenario integration, triggering the change of learning methods. The feature of virtual-real fusion of education Metaverse can realize seamless switching between real scenes, virtual scenes and virtual-reality fusion scenes, and can realize the teaching mode of multi-scene fusion, so that teachers can combine different scenes with specific teaching tasks and teaching objectives, in different situations. In-scenario transitions carry out seamless teaching to meet the needs of learners in all-round learning. For example, teachers can link classrooms, training rooms, internship companies and other learning scenarios at any time, and impart professional knowledge, practical skills and social practice to students in suitable scenarios. Each reaction of students can be turned into a concrete symbol. For example, if a student expresses doubts about the teacher's explanation, a question mark will pop up on his head, which is convenient for the teacher to capture feedback in time, and form interaction and communication with students in a timely manner. In the multi-scene teaching situation built, the knowledge in the book is directly restored and upgraded in the virtual world, the knowledge points in the book are changed from plane to three-dimensional, and presented in front of students, which is also conducive to stimulating students' hearing, vision and touch, etc. Sensory functions, mobilize students' enthusiasm for learning, stimulate students' learning motivation and improve students' learning outcomes.

Connect with market demand and promote in-depth cooperation between schools and enterprises. The Education Metaverse will promote the close integration of the virtual world and the real world, share economic, social and identity systems, and provide a platform for in-depth cooperation between schools and enterprises. Education Metaverse breaks the constraints of the real environment on school-enterprise cooperation and the integration of industry and education, provides rich educational resources, realistic practical situations, promotes the integration of engineering and learning, and solves the problem of disconnection between knowledge and skills teaching and work training; it reduces school-enterprise training for enterprises. The resources occupied by cooperation avoid the fireplace phenomenon in school-enterprise cooperation. Education is a complex social activity and a practical activity between people. However, due to differences in individual students' genetics, family education, social environment and subjective initiative, students have differences in the development of physical and psychological qualities, and imbalance. The in-depth integration of school-enterprise cooperation provides students with personalized learning options, so that students can arrange learning according to their own interests, abilities, and time, and tailor-made learning plans that meet their own conditions. Difficult knowledge points can be repeated at will. Knowledge points can be expanded and deepened arbitrarily, and equipment operation and practical simulation can be carried out according to their own needs, so as to increase the frequency of work-study alternation, realize the transformation and integration of theoretical knowledge and practical skills, and strengthen their professional skills.

Enhance the sense of identity and attractiveness of vocational education. Vocational education requires more than the blessing of advanced technical equipment. If there is no institutional support such as good career prospects, good social identity, good reputation and household registration, then vocational colleges are still unattractive to most people. Through the combination of reality and virtuality, the education Metaverse can reshape social concepts, reconstruct social identity, and make up for the gap in the social identity of professional talents to a certain extent. Moreover, Education Metaverse can also break through the limitations of physical space and choose to conduct internships in different companies according to their majors, hobbies and career plans, creating opportunities for students to simulate multiple careers, increasing students' professional experience, and helping students. Choose the right major and occupation.

4   The Risk of Applying Metaverse to Vocational Education

The educational Metaverse has a wide range of applications, but education is different from other fields of society. Vocational schools are faced with students who have not yet reached adulthood or who have just grown up. Their values have not yet formed and their minds have not yet matured. The educational Metaverse is not limited in time and space.

Mass information transmission and virtual reality interaction can easily lead to self-lost among vocational school students. Therefore, whether the technology of the educational Metaverse is mature, what are the security and normative issues behind data-driven, and whether there are other potential risks need further exploration.

4.1 Privacy Risk

Entering the Metaverse stage, various application scenarios will comprehensively collect and use social data in the physical world, accurately map life scenarios in the physical world to the virtual world, and continue to generate massive amounts of data. Data elements have become an important part of the social governance system. Digital governance has become the basic form of social governance, and big data has become a new factor of social production. Most of the current application software will monitor the entire process of browsing records, call records, and chat records, and data trading occurs from time to time. If the brain-computer interface technology is mature, it can enter the human body like a nano-robot, and the brain wave data will become information and be resold. Although the digital identity authentication function is conducive to clarifying the attribution of responsibility, this ultra-complete record of information also has certain disadvantages. Once some sensitive and private personal information is leaked, it will violate personal privacy. This method snatch the so-called top students, resulting in unfair new education.

4.2 Ethical Risks

The combination of emerging technologies and traditional vocational education brings new changes to its teaching methods, teacher-student relationship, teaching reform, and learning evaluation. Ethics bring shocks.How learners will establish correct worldviews and values in different cultural output and false information, in the virtual digital world, students' privacy protection, mental health, Internet addiction, cyberbullying, cultural erosion, ideology and ethics, etc. The problem has become an important issue facing the development of vocational education. In the absence of perfect rules and order, a decentralized educational Metaverse may lead to addiction risks that are difficult to regulate, which in turn threatens real learning and life. It is also necessary to fully consider ethical issues such as the role replacement between the learner's ID and virtual self, and the collaboration between teachers and virtual teachers.

4.3 Risk of Addiction

Starting from the human perceptual system, the application of multimedia, algorithmic images, installation art, projection interaction and other technologies creates a real experience for users, which makes people immersive and has a natural addiction. Moreover, students in vocational colleges are still young and have poor self-control. It is easy to spend too much time on technical experience and form spiritual dependence. If things go on like this, individuals will not be able to distinguish between reality and virtuality, and misuse the rules of the virtual world for the real world. In China, there are problems such as value distortion, or use technology as a means of escaping reality, indulging in the virtual world, refusing to assume social responsibilities in the real world, and encountering multiple crises such as identity, emotion, and cognition.

5 The Suggestions for Promoting the High-Quality Development of Vocational Education

In the process of building a digital China, managers of vocational education must keep a clear head, clearly recognize the potential risks of the education Metaverse, and ensure that teaching process management, teaching business management, teaching quality management and teaching monitoring management are clear and clear, and have the ability to implement them. It is possible to truly realize the improvement of the teaching quality of vocational education. To this end, it is necessary to deploy from a forward-looking perspective, strengthen top-level design, improve data standards and responsibility confirmation mechanisms, build educational data centers with multi-party educational entities, and promote the sharing, application and even research of educational data, so as to form clear rights and responsibilities, The process is clear, the governance process can be tested, traceable, open, and the educational subjects can be clearly arranged, the data rights of the multi-party subjects participating in education management are confirmed, the educational process is scientifically standardized, and a systematic educational governance with both available and safe data is formed. The model can effectively avoid the potential risks in the process of integrating the Metaverse and vocational education.

First of all, adhere to overall planning and advance in stages, and promote the application of Metaverse in vocational education from conception to reality. In the process of human information technology change, the barbaric growth of technology caused by the lack of overall top-level design has brought many hidden dangers and caused many negative impacts on social life. Therefore, the in-depth integration of the Metaverse and vocational education cannot be achieved overnight. It should be guided by the core socialist values, regulate and constrain the construction of the educational Metaverse from the legal level, moderately integrate in stages, and consciously construct educational scenes.

Secondly, guide the establishment of the governance principle of science and technology for good, and build an ethical supervision framework and system. Although the Metaverse will bring many new changes to vocational education, the essence of vocational education has not changed. Quality talents. It is necessary to adhere to the guidance of mainstream values, create a positive energy Metaverse scene according to the actual needs of the vocational education field, and achieve positive positive benefits. The invention, creation and use of technology all carry human values. Issues such as the equality of identities in the participation of multiple subjects in application scenarios, whether digital avatars have citizenship, and the mechanism for mutual recognition of credit banks still need to be continuously explored. Strengthen the supervision of teachers and students over the whole process of the education Metaverse resource system, maintain the transparency of the algorithm and improve the openness, strengthen the transparency of the operation practice of algorithm recommendation from the aspects of legislation, system and rules, and guide educators and learners to consciously abide by them Transparent ethical norms, thus promoting the continuous improvement of the algorithmic ethics supervision framework and system of the Learning Metaverse.

Finally, in the process of deep integration of the education metaworld and vocational education, the school information system and mechanism are constantly improved to build a fully functional digital campus. In order to ensure the smooth and orderly promotion of the application of education cloud universe in vocational education, it is necessary to clarify the information organization, the concept, vision and management basis of school information technology, so as to make the construction of new technologies and new scenes regular. Standardized internal information work methods and procedures are gradually formed to ensure the orderly implementation of the implementation process and prevent data leakage, value leading deviation and other problems.

Acknowledgements. This research was supported by the project of Research on the Transformation of Vocational Education Talent Training Model under the New Ecological Background of Digital Economy Employment (No. SZIIT2021SK008).

References

1. New Media Research Center, School of Journalism and Communication: Tsinghua University. 2020–2021 Metaverse Development Research Report. (2021-09-22) [2021-12-16]
2. Xiaheng, Z., Xiang, L.: Research status, hot spots and enlightenment of foreign Metaverse field. Ind. Econ. Rev. **2**, 199–214 (2022)
3. Ruijia, W.: Metaverse technology empowers physical education——exploration of theoretical framework, application scenario and technical route. Sch. Phys. Educ. **07**, 186–189 (2022)
4. Nan, X., Metaverse, E.: The future direction of teaching reform in vocational schools. China Vocat. Tech. Educ. **14**, 48–53 (2022)
5. Yawen, W., Li, Y., Changyuan, W., Guohui, W.: Discussion on experimental teaching in the field of education Metaverse. High. Eng. Educ. Res. **4**, 96–101 (2022)
6. Jiajun, Z., Junzi, Y.: On the interpretation and construction of learning space under the empowerment of intelligent technology. J. Dist. Educ. **39**(4), 62–71 (2021)
7. Li, H., Wang, W.: Digital twin intelligent learning space: connotation, model and strategy. Mod. Distance Educ. Res. **33**(3), 73–80+90 (2021)
8. Yan, W., Xin, Z.: The potential and challenges of education metaverse in vocational education. Vocat. Educ. **12**, 85–90 (2022)
9. Geping, L., Gao Nan, H., Hanlin, Q.Y., Metaverse, E.: Features, mechanisms and application scenarios. Open Educ. Res. **1**, 24–32 (2022)
10. Chen, S.-Y., Liu, S.-Y.: Using augmented reality to experiment with elements in a chemistry course. Comput. Hum. Behav. **111**, 106418 (2020)
11. Sahin, D., Yilmaz, R.M.: The effect of augmented reality technology on middle school students' achievements and attitudes towards science education. Comput. Educ. **144**, 103710 (2020)
12. Chang, S.-C., Hwang, G.-J.: Impacts of an augmented reality-based flipped learning guiding approach on students' scientific project performance and perceptions. Comput. Educ. **125**, 226–239 (2018)
13. Tzanavaris, S., Nikiforos, S., Mouratidis, D., Kermanidis, K.L.: Virtual learning communities (VLCs) rethinking: from negotiation and conflict to prompting and inspiring. Educ. Inf. Technol. **1**, 257–278 (2021)
14. The Stanford Daily. Stanford launches first class taught completely in virtual reality. https://www.stanforddaily.com/2021/12/01/stanford-launches-first-class-taught-completely-in-virtual-reality/

15. Bolger, R.K.: Finding wholes in the Metaverse: post human mystics as agents of evolutionary contextualization. Religions **12**(9), 1–15 (2021)
16. Chung, H.K.: Metaverse friend making system design and implement. J. Semicond. Display Technol. **20**(3), 97–102 (2021)
17. Sparkes, M.: What is a Metaverse? New Sci. **245**(3348), 18 (2021)
18. StokelWalker, C.: Facebook is now meta but why, and what even is the Metaverse? New Sci. **252**(3359), 12 (2021)

The Application Research of Education Metaverse Under the Framework of SWOT Analysis

Chunyan Jiang and Jinhong Xu[✉]

School of Finance and Economics, ShenZhen Institute of Information Technology, ShenZhen 518172, China
cyjiang@szu.edu.cn, 3383199759@qq.com

Abstract. Education Metaverse provides new development directions and pursuit goals for the new education model in the future. In fact, under the impact of the new crown pneumonia epidemic, the advantages of Education Metaverse are reflected. Education Metaverse provides teachers, students, enterprises and participants. New possibilities for living and learning. This article analyzes the fusion of the metaverse and education in thought, technology, scene, and body, and conducts a SWOT analysis of the metaverse on education. It is found that the education metaverse is a driving metaverse that combines the needs of reality, market to demand, individual needs and the needs of the larger environment. Provide an immersive, authentic, interactive, innovative, diverse, and collaborative education metaverse, which can effectively to promote education and teaching, as well as reform and innovation, which has a better role in promoting the future development of education. Grasping the integration between the metaverse and education can better open up, actively promote the development of the educational metaverse, expand the metaverse of education and teaching, the metaverse of the campus, the metaverse of the society, and promote the interdisciplinary of the educational metaverse, the excellent development of production-university-research and hybrid models.

Keywords: Metaverse · Education · SWOT · Learning Metaverse

1 Introduction

Under the outbreak and recovery of the global new crown pneumonia epidemic, the reduction of people's real-life activities has pushed the development of the metaverse to the front (Tzanavaris et al. 2021). Through the link of the virtual network, a series of activities of daily life are carried out on the network as much as possible. The important thing is that people have gradually adapted to this metaverse way of life, so that people can improve and improve the future metaverse. Updates create more and more expectations. At present, the metaverse is still a complex environment and mechanism that is constantly developing and evolving, especially in the first year of the metaverse in 2021, some famous companies have incorporated the elements of the metaverse into the overall

© The Author(s), under exclusive license to Springer Nature Switzerland AG 2022
L.-J. Zhang (Ed.): METAVERSE 2022, LNCS 13737, pp. 55–67, 2022.
https://doi.org/10.1007/978-3-031-23518-4_5

environment of the company. For example, Facebook changed to Meta and launched All in Metauniverse; Roblox is listed on the NYSE, igniting the concept of the metaverse with the title of "the first stock of the metaverse"; Axie Infinity is an online video game developed by Vietnamese studio Sky Mavis. Similarly, there are some countries in the world that particularly support the research and development of the metaverse, especially the metaverse is considered by the global industry to have an important impact on education. Meanwhile, the field of education is the main application field of the metaverse (Yoo et al. 2021). Learning the metaverse is a key and important part of the application of metaverse education, so all walks of life are actively marching towards metaverse education. Metaverse education can break the original education method, thereby creating new learning fields such as space, thinking, idea, environment, etc. To provide students and teachers with super comprehensive and perceptual shared resources, and to provide guarantee for high-quality education, teaching, and training models, it is very necessary to conduct in-depth discussions on the metaverse and education. In particular, what kind of promotion and impact will the fusion of the original universe and education bring to future education? What are the main aspects of the fusion between education and the metaverse? What dangers and challenges will the education metaverse face? What are the advantages and disadvantages of the educational metaverse? This has important theoretical value and practical significance.

2   Metaverse Definition, Origin, Development and Characteristics

2.1   Definition of the Metaverse

American science fiction writer Neil Stephenson (Stephenson 1992) first proposed the concept of the metaverse in Avalanche, and described the metaverse as a virtual urban environment parallel to real life. The metaverse is more complex (Smart et al. 2007), so far, the metaverse has not been clearly defined, but the metaverse is still an evolving concept, especially it is a variety of intelligent technologies and a variety of virtual and reality And a socialized form of the combination of the Internet. The "Metaverse Development Research Report 2020–2021" gives the following definition: "The metaverse is a new Internet application and social form that integrates the virtual and real worlds by integrating various new technologies. It provides an immersive experience based on extended display technology, generates a mirror image of the real world based on digital twin technology, builds an economic system based on blockchain technology, closely integrates the virtual world with the real world in economic system, social system and identity system, and allows each user produces content. Wikipedia explains the metaverse as "an online three-dimensional virtual environment used to describe the persistence and decentralization of the future. Metaverse builds a virtual world based on augmented reality technology to provide an immersive experience, generates a mirror world of the real world based on digital twin technology, builds an economic system based on blockchain technology, and integrates the virtual world with reality in the economic system, social system and identity system. The world is tightly coupled and allows each user to produce content and edit online. The concept of the metaverse is dualistic: it refers to a specific set of virtualization and 3D web technologies, and the way people see M's online life. Therefore, the metaverse cannot simply be regarded as a virtual space, but as a connection between the real world and the virtual world.

2.2 Juncture

The education metaverse can be understood as the integration of intelligent education in the cloud. Teachers and students participate in classrooms as digital identities and interact in virtual teaching places, and it is important that the metaverse focuses first on its social interactivity (Getchell et al. 2010).In the metaverse classroom, the introduction of VR equipment can fully reshape the presentation form of teaching content (Arvanitis et al. 2009; Cai et al. 2013), allowing students to "immerse" in knowledge. In addition, the plasticity of virtual space has also spawned scenarios such as virtual laboratory and virtual assembly, extending the metaverse from classroom to after-school activities. Especially under the catalysis of the new crown pneumonia epidemic, offline classroom education has stagnated, and online education has become the main field, which has to force the advancement and development of the education metaverse. Then the fusion of education and the metaverse is about to become a new innovation. But this innovation is full of difficulties and will be a hard road.

2.3 Educational Metaverse Features

Different definitions of the metaverse mean that people have different understandings of the metaverse, and then these understandings are a series of definitions based on the characteristics, shapes, states, conditions, etc. of the metaverse that they think and observe. Therefore, this paper also has a certain understanding of the characteristics of the metaverse. In order to meet people's in-depth communication, experience, learning, communication, connection, displays, and interactive, the metaverse is built through the integration of digital, artificial, intelligence, machine, network and the overall environment. The cosmic sphere, an ecological civilization space that integrates nature and society, has certain characteristics:

2.4 Interactivity

The education metaverse is first and foremost an intercommunication relationship, which connects teachers, students, knowledge content, learning environment, application scenarios and application purposes, and becomes a basic construction point of the education metaverse. They are the key of derivatives of the overall education metaverse. At the same time, these basic component points are connected, and after a certain link is changed, other basic component points are moved or changed or updated at any time, and the whole is integrated into an innovative metaverse teaching environment. Circumstances, mutual learning and communication, and through the feeling of the metaverse, to truly build and improve it.The interaction of the education metaverse is definitely manifested in different stages, which can open a new door for real education, according to different subject levels, field methods, environments, and locations, and create more optimized education and training models. Inject new soul into educational activities.

2.5 Synergy

Based on the above basic construction points, the education metaverse needs to establish a certain synergy. This synergy is constantly changing, perhaps changing anytime, anywhere. This synergy includes the synergy between technology and society, between teachers and students, between teachers and scenes, between students and scenes, between students and society, and so on. Today's education will face a series of problems, including technical problems and social needs. On the one hand, technical problems can promote learning efficiency, change students' learning methods, improve students' ability to diversify, improve teachers' teaching ability, and even a better educational environment can be created, but there are still some problems. The original breeding constructed with multiple conditions needs to reach a certain level under different conditions in order to support each other and promote each other. There is a certain degree of synergy between them, but there are also constraints.

2.6 Conjunctive

The purpose of the Education Metaverse is to better develop students' abilities, promote their development, and train students to become high-end or constructive talents needed by society and the country. Therefore, students, teachers and scenarios must be integrated enterprises, Society is bound up with each other. Individuals and institutions differ only in their entanglement, they do not exist as single elements (Barad 2007).This kind of conclusion is similar to building an ecosystem space, which can trigger the corresponding contracting relationship through different metaverse frameworks and space points, and place all participants in the metaverse space completely. To solve and face this network of conjugation, use corresponding digital conditions and evaluation criteria, and make corresponding adjustments in more dimensions of timely, effective and interactive spaces and scenes, thereby strengthening the degree of conjugative relationship and interaction.

2.7 Liquidity

The biggest feature of the education metaverse may be that it has strong fluidity. It may not have a given environment, nor a given condition, nor a fixed location. In the education metaverse, he can plan things according to the mood of his individual users, arrange to do what you want to do, or organize what you want to do. Education comes from the crowd. It can provide users with a particularly realistic and realistic environment. These real environments, including his psychological condition, physical condition or somatosensory behavior, are important for perception, and it is a kind of changing and real. A metaverse exploration of emotion and immersion. For example, he may feel a gust of wind coming out, or he can feel the environment like a real skydiving and feel weightless when skydiving, then he can feel immersive to explore and learn (Fig. 1).

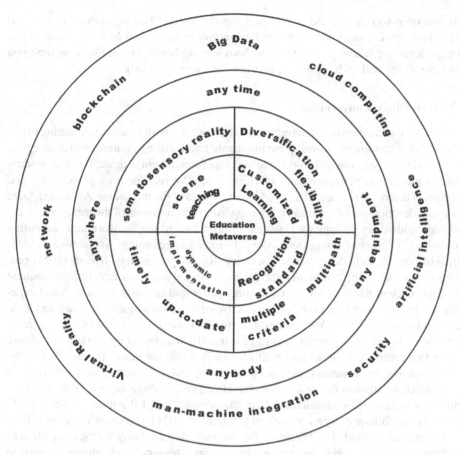

Fig. 1. Educational metaverse application scenario

3   Metaverse and Educational Fusion Goals

3.1   Fusion of Ideas

The unexpected arrival of the new crown pneumonia epidemic has caused huge changes in people's needs in life and society, especially based on the early stage, we have adopted electronic payment in the consuming process, and shopping is done through the Internet, then this has basically changed. People's requirements and conditions of life. It has also brought about dramatic changes in socially connected lifestyles as well as industrial organization and consumption patterns. Then this change of thinking is exactly the first generation of thinking of the metaverse. Hooks (1994) sees teaching as "the union of mind, body and spirit, not only to acquire knowledge in books, but also to acquire knowledge of how to live in the world. There is no doubt that the thinking of the metaverse is to integrate all environmental conditions and individual users into an overall virtual world under the premise of the Internet. Then this virtual world has a sense of body and cognition. It will create more favorable conditions for human beings and their work and life, and even you can handle everything properly without leaving home.It is this kind of thinking that connects education and the metaverse. Education Metaverse allows you to experience the learning experience without leaving home, and at the same time you can have all the real feelings in the process of learning knowledge.

3.2 Technology Convergence

The fusion of education and metaverse provides learners with innovative learning methods, learning conditions, learning environments and learning content, which integrate the virtual world and the real world, and integrate human beings through corresponding technologies, science, experiments, machines, etc. The real feelings, perceptions, and feelings of the metaverse are all mapped into the world of the metaverse. At present, there are many descriptions of the underlying supporting technologies of the metaverse in the industry, which can be roughly classified into six categories: network and computing technology, Internet of Things technology, blockchain technology, interactive technology, video game technology, and artificial intelligence technology. Radoff (2021) proposes a seven-layer metaverse architecture consisting of infrastructure, human-machine interface, decentralization, spatial computing, economic creation, discovery, and experience from the bottom up. From the perspective of development stages, Jonathan Glick, senior editor of The New York Times, believes that the development of the hyperuniverse consists of two stages: the first stage is mainly manifested by participants' desire to live in a completely virtual space, this Space is somehow more "beautiful" than the real world, and the advanced stage is the technological ecosystem that finally realizes the connection between fact and fiction (Hackl 2021). The three-layer framework of the education metaverse is summarized from the perspective of the macro – framework: infrastructure, interaction and ecosystem (Duan et al. 2021).The super virtual-real integration function provided by Metauniverse will provide a new way for the integration of teaching and learning environments, and realize cross-regional in-depth participation in learning, barrier-free distance collaborative learning exploration, verifiable experimental environment, and freely created group maker space, etc.

3.3 Scene Fusion

Education Metaverse is a digital and intelligent ecological environment built on the basis of advanced digital technology and science and technology mixed realization of brain-computer interface, blockchain, cloud computing and other new communication technologies. After using the metaverse, the intelligence field and enabling education can be combined to provide an excellent condition and environment for education. Especially in the process of education and teaching, it is a very important condition to effectively integrate knowledge, teaching, students' emotions and environment, so that students can receive knowledge quickly and effectively. In the current state, teachers improve learning efficiency by flipping classroom, online and offline mixed teaching and some open homework after class, but there will be certain restrictions and constraints in the learning process, so this situation will hinder classroom teaching. Effect, or weaken the ability of students to accept knowledge. Especially in the face of more abstract theories or mathematical models, then this situation will be more prominent. The creation and development of the metaverse will provide strong support for solving these teaching problems, and the Panoramic Learning Field will provide comprehensive support for the teaching and learning process of teachers and students (Barry et al. 2015). Panorama Xinchang is an educational metaverse or educational metaverse space created based on digital twins, Internet of Things, brain-computer interfaces and wearable devices to realize human-computer simulation communication (Diaz et al. 2020).With super social interaction, deep immersion, high fidelity, free creation and other functions, it provides comprehensive support for the learning process of learners. Students can use related equipment to enter the education metaverse, realize the deep integration and continuous development of teaching and learning activities before, during and after class, and support the learning process by creating a virtual and real learning environment. Lee (2021) found that existing research mainly focuses on topics such as the methods and effects of teaching resources, the application of virtual environments in language and cultural education, educational strategies based on the dual identities of students and virtual avatars, and the design and implementation of learning platforms. The Education Metaverse will provide critical support for equitable and quality education. Both students and teachers have access to quality educational opportunities from renowned university teachers. Those students in rural, remote areas, and ordinary universities can get the opportunity to use sophisticated experimental equipment and experience collaborative inquiry experiments.

3.4 Integration of Mind and Body

The unity of body and mind is a concept that education and teaching can achieve the best goal. If the body and mind accept one thing at the same time, then the overall body utility will be maximized, because human behavior is through the interaction between the brain, the body and the environment. As a result, the body's cognition will allow the brain to perceive the surrounding environment and interact with each other, resulting in a series of behaviors. Cognition and psychology, then through the body's senses and touch, which are transmitted to every nerve in the body, which has an important impact on the individual's ability to act or act. Therefore, in the process of educating the metaverse, he can integrate this perception and the individual's behavioral ability, and obtain from the virtual world what other realities do not have, or what reality can feel, in the virtual world, you can also feel the same feeling of reality. Bringing people into an environment where emotions are distributed, you and reality, then this meets the requirements of the unity of body and mind, especially under the conditions of individual media environment, culture, and social practice environment, people's cognition, there will be strong differences. With educational language, the internal characteristics of the individual and the influence of the external environment on the individual will be integrated together, so in an environment similar to real touch and feeling, the ability to learn and feel will be improved, and the ability to communicate what is in reality. Everything that happens can exist in the virtual world, so this just achieves the effect of teaching in the metalanguage.

4 Metaverse SWOT Analysis of Education

4.1 Strengths

Scene interaction. The biggest advantage of Education Metaverse is the interoperability scenarios. It can put forward diversified, diverse and multi-dimensional requirements for educational informatization through application scenarios, digital scenarios, system scenarios, and target scenarios, and comb through all scenarios. Incorporated into the educational metaverse scene. The scene contributed in this way has the same application level for any teacher, any individual student, or educational institution, social group, company, enterprise, etc., completely ignoring the problem of coordinate location, and it is fair to everyone.

The experience feels real. When teachers, students, educational institutions, and enterprises are all learning and active in the educational metaverse, educational research can bring the most authentic experience, just like being in an immersive classroom, and it can be constantly transformed Any classroom, any environment, and any conditions allow teachers and students to experience problems that cannot be solved instantaneously by the realistic environment brought by the education metaverse. In the education meta-verse, as long as you can imagine or ask for what needs, then the education metaverse can fulfill all your wishes. Vergne et al. (2019) designed a real-life escape room game called "Escape the Lab", which turned the learning process into exploration and revealing activities, allowing learners to become discoverers, researchers and explorers. Especially now that many students and teachers have a certain degree of social phobia, then in this case, this situation can be avoided through the education metaverse. In the virtual world, you can map your own situation or create a new one. A pattern to help you meet your needs.

Learning together inside and outside the classroom. Students and teachers can not only learn at the same time in the classroom, but also conduct decentralized learning. Instead of focusing on learning at one point in time, they can also learn the knowledge they want to acquire different points in time, and can incorporate knowledge points into the game, to learn subtly in the game. And in class, teachers can arrange homework and pass it to students through games. Students learn and do homework in games, which can improve students' acceptance and learning efficiency, and the transformation of knowledge will also be improved. The important thing is that some students have their own learning methods and models. Not all students have a unified standard. After the teacher has completed the course in the classroom, the students can extend or renew their knowledge points according to the content of the teacher's teaching. Learning, with better retrospective and predictive and prospective.

The content of education and teaching is diversified. The teaching content of the education metaverse needs to meet the aspects of new networks, new platform, new resource, new campus, new application and a new security. Teachers and students, as well as other participants, can continue to learn in a shared, standardized, creative, scalable, and perfectable educational metaverse, and you can continuously customize the response according to each person's own needs. In the traditional classroom, all students will have the same teaching content. But in the education metaverse, absolutely every student will choose the knowledge they want to acquire according to their own hobbies, creative points, and inspiration points, especially the knowledge points can be transformed into many small points, according to their own interests and hobbies. Select learning content.

Refined teaching. Adaptive feedback to individual learners based on ambient intelligence, including learning behavior adaptation, learning path guidance, learning process intervention, and learning resource push. Based on big data analysis, teachers are the most important factor to avoid "out of focus" in students' learning activities (Rospigliosi 2022). Teachers can continuously optimize and improve teaching design, teaching guidance and teaching decision-making to achieve accurate teaching supply.

4.2 Weaknesses

Student performance is diverse. The educational metaverse is a complex, free, diverse resource, multi-situation, and multi-application meta-universe educational world. Under this multi-condition and multi-rule situation, students must have a greater response difference. Theoretically, there is a large difference between students, which is a normal phenomenon for normal classroom and offline classroom education, but in the world of the metaverse, the difference between each student expands. In this case, when someone says that they need to refine, analyze, update and innovate the corresponding educational and teaching content suitable for each student, then the workload of the content of the metaverse will increase during the May Day, so for now, This is a relative disadvantage, but it could be an advantage in the future metaverse.

Teacher feedback is diverse and complex. The educational metaverse is about exploiting diverse knowledge and content to serve students and teachers as well as participants. However, this service will continue to develop more detailed and small conditions and guidelines according to the needs of students, teachers and other participants, the purpose is to meet their own needs and meet the needs of others. At the same time, students' demand for knowledge will give teachers more feedback, and teachers should update the corresponding content based on this feedback. But the content of this feedback will become more and more complicated. Updating this kind of content in the early educational originals may require a lot of manpower, material resources, and financial resources, but when the metaverse develops to a certain extent, this has turned into an advantage.

The complexity of the management system has increased. When the metaverse enters the public eye, it means that all real environments will be integrated, transformed, and innovated again with the virtual network environment. New, innovative and inclusive management systems are needed. This kind of management system must not only constrain reality, but also manage the principles of virtual education, then it will inevitably increase the complexity of the management system's setting and implementation, and in the process of continuous metaverse evolution, the complexity will deepen.

4.3 Opportunity

The realization of the education metaverse will bring earthshaking changes to education, and it is also a new round of education innovation. It is necessary to seize the opportunity and prepare for the development of the education metaverse.

Customized education. Since education comes from focusing on traditional teacher standards, teaching rules, training programs, training models, etc., there are mismatched characteristics. Therefore, it is necessary to formulate customized norms, standards, conditions, models, teaching methods based on the situation of one's own education metaverse, activity logic, etc. Then these can ensure the stable, safe and orderly operation of the education metaverse. In the current education principle, it has large data resources, so how can we seize the existing opportunities and put all the conditions and standards into the education park universe? and ensuring that everyone has a customizable education and training program is extremely important.

Industry standard specifies. In the educational principle, the needs of enterprises, social needs, teachers, students, and schools are all integrated, and corresponding industry standards are customized for different industries, different regions, different cities, etc., especially In order to better achieve the goal of education metaverse by providing corresponding solutions and measures according to the needs of different categories in the industry, and converting the original batch standardized content into both standard and specific content.

Liberalization of information sharing for determination and identification of non-uniform standards. Teachers can also shape the same types of beings as learners. It mainly includes: virtual teachers, that is, a real virtual image synthesized by intelligent technology, which can be freely "deformed" according to the needs of the teaching situation. Avatar teacher, that is, the teacher teaches in the form of an avatar; holographic teacher, that is, the teacher teaches in the form of a real mirror. With the use of the education park for a week, students can constantly switch the type of teacher, teaching method, teaching resources, teaching content, etc., so there will be non-uniform standards for judgment and informatization criteria for identification.

4.4   Threat

The limitation and elimination of ideological value system and morality. There is a big difference between the social activities of the education system and other systems, especially in the education assistance activities, the ideological and behavior of various participants will change greatly, which may appear in real life and the virtual world. There is a huge difference. Virtual worlds also have ethics. The government and all sectors of society should shoulder the responsibility of regulating cyberspace, ensuring the security of cyberspace and preventing technology abuse. Education originates from a constructed world that attaches great importance to the digital nature based on intelligent algorithms. Diversified applications and analysis are carried out through numbers, but how to transmit the correct ideological value system and build corresponding moral standards through this form is an A question worth pondering. Especially in the process of education principles, various actors will show their own thinking patterns and behavior patterns, then it will affect the thinking, behavior of other participating individuals at the same time, then this will cause certain security risks, no matter what. Whether it is ideological or behavioral, it will induce problems in other individuals in society. If this happens, how to restrict or limit the ideological value system and moral problems has become a very important and urgent problem to be solved.

Threats posed by immature technology. Although the education metaverse has gained a certain level and recognition on the underlying basis, it still has many technical difficulties that need to be broken through, especially in the current process of immersion and integration between the virtual environment and the offline environment. Under the condition that the machine switching is not natural and convenient enough, various operations are cumbersome and cannot be transferred with the change of consciousness, then the requirements for the design and application of the software, the surrounding WiFi, the network environment and the data environment are all Relatively high, including data system, identity system, economic system and integration of domestic and foreign systems and so on. So this has a certain weakening phenomenon for the educational metaverse, and if this problem cannot be solved, then it is a very important threat to educational reasons.

Threats to data security. The Education Metaverse has huge data resources. This data resource includes data acquisition, data transmission, data import, export, etc., then these components are subject to technological development, as well as the ability to acquire and transform data. The trader universe, if he is a characterizing data, needs to describe all the content into a set of data processes that can be converted at any time according to the environmental conditions at different time points, and this situation needs to be updated and improved in time. At the same time, the reason why different countries will develop their own systems is the system, so how to uniformly summarize, identify, transmit, and then give feedback on the reasons of different countries is very difficult. Once these problems are not solved or there is neglect, then there will be a problem of data loss and even leakage of secrets.

Education and teaching depth is not enough. The current education metaverse is in a primary state, and only some exchanges are carried out through VR or some online interactive demonstrations, so the interaction between teachers and teachers is far from the interaction between classroom education and interaction between students. Not enough, it is necessary to continuously strengthen the update of the course content. The expansion of the course training model is based on the course content in the metaverse and the development of some innovative thinking methods and thinking courses. Learning resources and teaching applications that are more suitable for multimodal environmental content, knowledge structure, and activity games in the educational metaverse should be introduced.

Threats posed by inadequate assessment mechanisms. The education park universe is in the primary research and development state, and its application in the field of education is also advancing. So how can we better evaluate whether an education park universe is suitable for the current education situation and other mutual influencing factors? In general, it is extremely important, that is to say, teachers and students, good social units, etc. must be integrated with information network platform resources, and the scattered content must be merged into a complete system, in order to bring the educational principles into play. In order to maximize the utility, how to integrate them together is extremely important, and how to formulate a corresponding evaluation criterion is even more important (Fig. 2).

Fig. 2. Shows the strengths, weaknesses, opportunities and threats of SWOT analysis

5 Metaverse Summary and Outlook

To sum up, it can be seen that the education metaverse is a driving metaverse that combines the needs of reality, market demand, individual needs and the needs of the larger environment. The education metaverse is a diverse, multimodal and multi-scenario metaverse universe. Especially the education metaverse, it can make students and teachers feel the difference of educational knowledge in depth, and can combine situational teaching, personalized learning, gamification learning, teacher independent learning and teacher integrated learning in a variety of scenarios. At the same time, it can also provide an immersive, authentic, interactive, innovative, diverse, and collaborative education metaverse, which can effectively promote education, reform, and innovation, and has a better role in promoting the future development of education. Grasping the integration between the metaverse and education can better open up, actively promote the development of the educational metaverse, expand the metaverse of education and teaching, the metaverse of the campus, the metaverse of the society, and promote the interdisciplinary of the educational metaverse, the excellent development of production-university-research and hybrid models.

Acknowledgements. This research was supported by Research on the Influence Path and Action Mechanism of Enterprise Financialization on the Balanced Development of the Real Economy under the Background of Economic Uncertainty (No. SZIIT2022SK009); Research on the High Quality Development of Shenzhen Industrial System under the New Development Pattern of Double Cycle (No. SZIIT2021SK010).

References

Arvanitis, T.N., et al.: Human factors and qualitative pedagogical evaluation of a mobile augmented reality system for science education used by learners with physical disabilities. Pers. Ubiquit. Comput. **13**(3), 243–250 (2009)

Barad, K.: Meeting the Universe Halfway: Quantum Physics and the Entanglement of Matter and Meaning, p.66, p. 33. Duke University Press, Durham, NC (2007)

Barry, D.M., et al.: Evaluation for students' learning manner using eye blinking system in Metaverse. Procedia Comput. Sci. **60**, 1195–1204 (2015)

Cai, S., Chiang, F.-K., Wang, X.: Using the augmented reality 3D technique for a convex imaging experiment in a physics course. Int. J. Eng. Educ. **4**, 856–865 (2013)

Diaz, J.E.M., Saldaña, D., Andrés, C., Alberto, C.: Virtual world as a resource for hybrid education. Int. J. Emerg. Technol. inLearning **15**(15), 94–109 (2020)

Getchell, K., Oliver, I., Miller, A., Allison, C.: Metaverses as a platform for game based learning. In: 2010 24th IEEE International Conference on Advanced Information Networking and Applications, pp. 1195–1202 (2010). https://doi.org/10.1109/AINA.2010.125

Hooks, B.: Teaching to Transgress: Education as the Practice of Freedom, p. 15. Routledge, New York (1994)

Lee, J.Y.: A study on Metaverse hype for sustainable growth. Int. J. Adv. Smart Convergence **10**(3), 72–80 (2021)

Lekova, A., Dimitrova, M., Kostova, S., Bouattane, O., Ozaeta, L.: BCI for assessing the emotional and cognitive skills of children with special educational needs. In: 2018 IEEE 5th International Congress on Information Science and Technology (CiSt), pp. 400-403 (2018). https://doi.org/10.1109/CIST.2018.8596571

Martin, G.F.: The social and psychological impact of musical collective creative processes in virtual environments; The Avatar Orchestra Metaverse in Second Life. Music/Technol. **11**(12), 75–87 (2018)

Facebook is set to become a metaverse company-what could that mean for society? 19 Nov 2021. https://www.Weforum.org/agenda/2021/10/facebook-is-set-to-become-a-meta-verse-company-what-could-that-mean-for-society (2021)

Ning, H., et al.: A survey on meta-verse; the state-of-the-art, technologies, applications, and challenges. arXiv preprint arXiv:2111.09673 (2021)

Perdana, I., Usop, L.S., Cakranegara, P.A., Linarto, L., Arifin, A.: Teacher educators perspectives on the use of augmented reality for foreign languageL. JTP-Jurnal 'Teknologi Pendidi-kan **23**(2), 112–128 (2021)

Rospigliosi, P.A.: Metaverse or simulacra? roblox, minecraft, meta and the turn to virtual reality for education, socialization and work. Interact. Learn. Environ. **30**(1), 1–3 (2022)

Smart, J., Cascio, J., Paffendorf, J.: Metaverse roadmap: pathway to the 3D web [Internet]. Acceleration Studies Foundation, Ann Arbor (MI) (2007). https://www.metaverseroadmap.org/MetaverseRoadmapOverview.pdf

Stephenson, N.: Snow Crash, p. 63. Bantam Books, New York (1992)

Steven, S., Alan, S., Zak, P., Ernest, C.D.D.L.: Ready Player One. Warner Bros, USA (2018)

Tzanavaris, S., Nikiforos, S., Mouratidis, D., Lida Kermanidis, K.: Virtual learning communities (VLCs) rethinking: from negotiation and conflict to prompting and inspiring. Educ. Inf. Technol. **1**, 257–278 (2021)

The Research of Medical Metaverse Application Under the Background of the Normalization of the New Crown Epidemic

Jinhong Xu[✉], Chunyan Jiang, Wei Wei, and Yi Li

ShenZhen Institute of Information Technology, ShenZhen 518172, People's Republic of China
21871744@qq.com

Abstract. At present, the traditional medical model is facing the prominent contradiction of the imbalance between supply and demand, and under the new background of the normalization of the new crown epidemic, the development of medical care is facing the transformation needs of prevention and control work, work focus and development concept. In order to explore the feasibility and application scenarios of the application of the Metaverse in the medical field under the background of the normalization of the epidemic, this paper studied the development status of the Metaverse in the medical field and its application advantages through the literature method, and finds that the development of the Metaverse shows two trends: on the one hand, it is from real to virtual, to realize the digitization of real experience, on the other hand, from virtual to real, to realize the realization of digital experience, through the perfect connection between virtual and reality, will create the next new era of medical information interconnection. The immersive environment of the Metaverse world and the integration of virtual and real space and the characteristics of hyper-simulation plays an important role in realizing disease visualization, famous doctors, psychotherapy scenarios, and innovative pension models. Based on the research and judgment of the advantages of the Metaverse in the medical field, the scenarios or paths of the Metaverse in medical applications are mainly reflected in five aspects: clinical surgery, medical robots, medical teaching, drug and medical device research and development, and AI super doctors.

Keywords: Metaverse · Medical · Normalization of the new crown epidemic · AI · AR/VR · Scenario

1 Introduction

As the latest form of the Internet, the Metaverse is a hybrid of the Internet, 5G and virtual fusion technology, and a synthesis of virtual reality technology. It connects the virtual world with the physical world, includes the network, hardware terminals and users, and creates an immersive learning environment, and the virtual world will not only be a visual experience, but also a comprehensive sensory experience of virtual vision, real vision, hearing, and touch. The development of the Metaverse presents a trend of two aspects:

© The Author(s), under exclusive license to Springer Nature Switzerland AG 2022
L.-J. Zhang (Ed.): METAVERSE 2022, LNCS 13737, pp. 68–80, 2022.
https://doi.org/10.1007/978-3-031-23518-4_6

on the one hand, it is from real to virtual to realize the digitization of real experience, on the other hand, it is from virtual to real, to realize the realization of digital experience, through the perfect connection between virtual and reality, it will create the next new era of information interconnection. Nowadays, many industries have invested in the exploration of the Metaverse, and the application of the health and medical industry has begun to emerge.

The traditional medical model faces the outstanding challenge of the imbalance between supply and demand, and under the challenge of the normalization of the new crown epidemic, the future Metaverse is expected to reconstruct the medical system to achieve the development vision of universal health. Through the analysis of the development status of the medical field in China and the analysis of the concept and characteristics of the Metaverse, this paper analyzes the natural advantages of the Metaverse introducing the medical field, and explores the application of the Metaverse in the medical field.

2 Medical Development Status

At present, the contradiction between supply and demand of China's traditional medical model is prominent. On the one hand, although the supply of medical resources has made great progress compared with the past, there is still a big gap compared with developed countries, which is mainly manifested in insufficient investment in medical funds, poor quality of medical services, and low efficiency of the medical system, which makes it difficult for China's medical system to meet the growing medical needs of our people. In addition, the normalization of the global new crown virus epidemic has put forward new requirements for people's daily life and work styles, the focus of medical and health undertakings, and the conceptual change of government-related work.

2.1 The Short Board of Medical Resource Supply is Obvious

2.1.1 Medical Capital Investment has not Maintained a Synchronous Increase with Fiscal Revenue

According to the "2021 Statistical Bulletin on the Development of China's Health and Health Undertakings", the total national health expenditure in 2021 is estimated to be 7,559.36 billion yuan, of which: the government health expenditure is 2,071.85 billion yuan, accounting for 27.4%; Social health expenditure was 3,392.03 billion yuan, accounting for 44.9%; Personal health expenditure was 2,095.48 billion yuan, accounting for 27.7%. The total per capital expenditure on health is 5348. 1 yuan, and the total expenditure on health accounts for 6.5% of GDP. China's medical and health resources, whether in terms of total amount or per capital, still have a big gap compared with developed countries, and health development lags behind economic development. Since 1995, the Chinese government's health budget has grown at an average annual rate of 14.2 percent, compared with 17.5 percent for government revenue over the same period. Social investment has not kept pace with government revenues.

By the end of 2021, the total number of medical and health institutions in the country 1030935, an increase of 8,013 over the previous year. Among them, there are 36,570 hospitals, 977,790 primary medical and health institutions, and 13,276 professional public health institutions (Fig. 1).

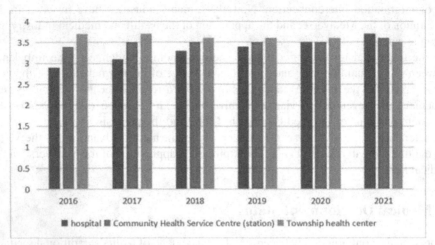

Fig. 1. Number of hospitals, community health service centers (stations) and township health centers in China (unit: 10,000)

There are 9.448 million beds in medical and health institutions nationwide, including 7.413 million in hospitals (78.5%), 1.712 million in primary medical and health institutions (18. 1%), and 302,000 in professional public health institutions (3.2%).

From the overall point of view, the irrational distribution of medical resources in China still exists, and the top three hospitals with higher grades have high-quality medical services and management, medical quality and medical efficiency, and can continuously absorb high-quality doctors, high-quality cooperation platforms and other high-quality resources, and the popularity brought by this further attracts a large number of patients to come to seek medical treatment, so the siphon effect leads to patients getting together, the gap between urban and rural medical resources and services is large, and the sinking of resources is facing resistance.

2.1.2 The Quality of Medical and Health Resources Needs to be Improved

By the end of 2021, the total number of health personnel in the country was 13.983 million, an increase of 508,000 over the previous year (an increase of 3.8%). Among them, there are 11.242 million health technicians. Among the health technicians, there are 4.287 million practicing (assistant) physicians and 5.018 million registered nurses.

According to the "National Medical and Health Service System Planning Outline (2015—2020)", the number of practicing (assistant) physicians, nurses and beds per 1,000 population is relatively low. Among practicing (assistant) physicians, only 45% have a bachelor's degree or above; Among the registered nurses, only 10% have a bachelor's degree or above. At the same time, from the perspective of the high-end medical device market, especially the third-class hospitals in first- and second-tier cities, foreign capital accounts for the vast majority of the proportion, and even reaches more than 90% (Fig. 2).

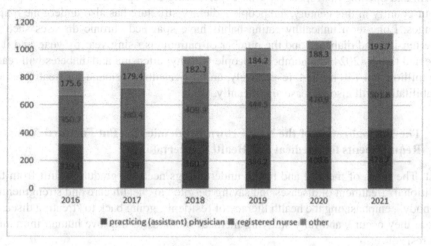

Fig. 2. Number of health technicians in the country (unit: 10,000 people)

2.2 The Demand for Medical Resources from Our People is Increasing day by day

In recent years, with the improvement of per capita income and people's health aware-ness, people have paid more attention to the prevention of diseases, which has brought about the growing rigid demand of the medical industry.

2.2.1 Increase in Population Ageing

With the advancement of medical technology, the average life expectancy of the global population continues to increase, which also brings about the problem of population aging that cannot be ignored. The number of people over the age of 65 in China has increased from 130 million in 2013 to 190 million in 2020, and the proportion of the total population has also increased from 9.7% to 13.5%, from the total amount and relative quantity, the growth trend is extremely obvious, and China's aging problem is intensifying, becoming a social problem that has to be faced.

2.2.2 High Incidence of Intractable Diseases such as Cancer

Due to the increasing complexity of the current human living environment, the incidence of intractable diseases such as cancer has generally increased. In 2015, there were 4 million new cases of cancer in China, and by 2020, the number has reached 4.6 million, and it is expected to grow to 5.2 million by 2025.

2.2.3   Growing Demand for Chronic Diseases and Rehabilitation

With the continuous improvement of the people's living standards since the beginning of reform and opening up, especially after experiencing the rapid economic development of our country in this century, the people's dietary structure has also undergone major changes. Long-term unhealthy eating habits have spawned chronic diseases such as hypertension and diabetes, and the number of patients is rising year by year, and it is expected that by 2024, the number of people with hypertension and diabetes will reach 380 million and 130 million, respectively, and the resulting demand for treatment and rehabilitation will also increase significantly.

2.3   The Normalization of the New Crown Epidemic Has Put Forward New Requirements for Medical and Health Undertakings

First, The focus of medical and health undertakings needs to gradually shift from the traditional "treatment of diseases and saving people" to "health care and strengthening the body", emphasizing the health literacy of residents, going back to "treating diseases before they occur", and fully studying medical methods to improve human immunity and resistance;

Second, living and behavior habits will be changed greatly. Wearing masks, shopping online, reducing social gatherings, and contactless takeaways will become routine. Health care services should actively respond to changes in people's living, working styles and habits, and update service content and service methods;

Third, the concept of health needs to be systematically and comprehensively integrated into the various plans of social governance and management, and the goal of universal health should be incorporated into various public policies. This also puts forward requirements for the change of the concept of government public management, including public utilities such as medical and health services.

3   The Concept and Characteristics of the Medical Metaverse

3.1   The Concept of the Medical Metaverse

Currently, there are different definitions of the Metaverse. Through the literature method, the author concludes that the Metaverse is a high-level form of the Internet, a comprehensive platform for creation, trading, socialization, entertainment, and display, and a perfect channel connecting online and offline. Then, the concept of medical Metaverse should be based on the Internet, big data, 5G and virtual fusion technology and other technologies as the support, through the doctor's vision, touch and other pluralistic ways to perceive a virtual and real medical ecological space created by various technical means.

3.2   Basic Caracteristics of the Medical Metaverse

In view of the main characteristics of the Metaverse, such as "deep immersion", "hyper-simulation", "virtual and real space" and "interactive integration", the author believes that the medical Metaverse should have the following main characteristics:

3.2.1 Virtual-real Fusion

The Metaverse simulates the real world through digital technology, constructing a "digital twin" world that contains two symbiotic forms of real-world boke and virtual world self-creation. In the medical Metaverse world, users can wear medical devices and medical equipment, immersive medical treatment, to achieve the same effect of offline treatment or even better effect, the treatment of mental illness may be more miraculous. Not only can you create the things imagined in your own mind by concretizing abstract thinking, but also give individual emotions in the virtual world, reflect the will of real people, and realize the synchronization of online and offline communication, thereby improving the quality of communication between individuals in the medical Metaverse, so that the medical Metaverse can both approximate real life and transcend real life.

3.2.2 Open Creation and Communication

In the medical Metaverse space, each user can freely enter the space at any place and time to create social relations and scenes that meet their own needs, and the communication scenario will also revolve around the user itself, which is a decentralized and near-equal communication pattern. At the same time, medical Metaverse users can also carry out various social activities between doctors and patients, patients and doctors in the space of the Metaverse, which not only achieves the real social and emotional experience provided by panoramic social perception, but also hopes to form a safer and more harmonious doctor-patient relationship. The visualization and visualization of medical terms can greatly improve the patient"s cognition and understanding of the disease, and achieve synchronous and effective real-time communication.

3.2.3 Intelligent Digital Collections

Relying on digital technologies such as artificial intelligence, Blockchain, MR and the Internet of things, Metaverse includes cyberspace, big data world and virtual reality world, and is a collection of intelligent digital technologies. The same is true of the medical Metaverse. For example, through big data technology, it captures system data such as user health care and pension as the original basis for personalized medicine; Through AR and other technologies, we ensure the immersive experience and interaction of various senses such as vision, hearing, and touch after entering the Metaverse; Through 5G technology and cloud computing, large-scale users can enter the medical Metaverse at the same time, solve the problems of "difficult to see a doctor", "medical service supply is in short supply", and ensure the fluency of users' simultaneous use. And with the continuous expansion of the Metaverse technology collection, more advanced technologies and innovative applications will also be added to the service scope of the medical meta-universe.

3.2.4 Online and Offline Integration

The deep integration of virtualization and real in the Metaverse forms an online and offline integration relationship, and the boundary between virtual and reality in the Metaverse space will no longer be clear, and individuals will exist in an online form, in which various life and social activities will be carried out to meet their offline needs. The emergence of the medical Metaverse will promote the comprehensive integration of online and offline and form a new type of social relationship. Online medical consultation + general practitioners come to the door, online user personalized data + daily life care robots and other online and offline combination punches, which are of great practical significance for the elderly, especially the single elderly, in their life, and can ensure their basic social needs and learning and life needs.

4 The Current Status of the Metaverse in the Field of Medicine

4.1 New Technologies is Rich in Various Applications in the Medical Field

On one hand, new technologies in the Metaverse field such as VR virtual reality and AR augmented reality are being used more in the medical industry. At present, it is mainly to solve the problem of human-machine integration. Taking the laparoscopic minimally invasive surgery support system as an example, the wounds of the current new minimally invasive surgery is very small, but because the information inside the minimally invasive surgery cannot be seen by the host physician, it is necessary to use the endoscope to register the data taken by the preoperative CT and guide the operation through virtual reality simulation.

On the other hand, the urgent clinical demand for precision medicine has spawned the application of AI artificial intelligence technology in the medical field. This includes early CADe (Computer-assisted detection) computer-aided testing, which can effectively reduce the rate of missed diagnoses in clinical care; There is also CADx (Computer-assisted diagnosis) computer-aided diagnosis, which can also greatly reduce the rate of misdiagnosis. Based on the application of Metaverse technology such as AI artificial intelligence, intelligent detection, intelligent classification, and intelligent segmentation of images can be carried out, and auxiliary diagnosis solutions can be provided through multi-modal information fusion big data analysis, which helps to greatly improve the accuracy of diagnosis and achieve precision medicine.

4.2 The Era of Imaging Big Data Promotes Changes in the Medical Field

With the continuous growth of people's demand for medical treatment, the current demand for image detection has doubled, and the number of image detection has increased year by year, resulting not only bringing a large demand for detection equipment, but also bringing great challenges to the data storage equipment, a CT examination will acquire more than 6,000 images, a patient may also do a variety of examinations, after each film to transfer all the data to the server, and finally to the storage device.These processes will bring massive amounts of data, and these processes occur all the time in the hospital, this "era of image big data" puts forward high requirements for storage devices.

In the era of imaging big data, all kinds of medical images are stored in PACS, all kinds of clinical information is stored in HIS, all kinds of examination and test information are stored in LIS, and the preservation requirements of these data are long-term retention of online for three years and offline for three years. According to the available data, the current annual growth rate of medical imaging data in the United States is 63. 1%, and the annual growth rate of radiologists is only 2.2%, a gap of 60.9%; The annual growth rate of imaging data in China is 30%, and the annual growth rate of radiologists is 4. 1%, and the gap is 23.9%. Therefore, relying only on the doctor's human eye to observe the huge image is facing a huge challenge, which brings huge development space to the Metaverse technology represented by AI artificial intelligence.

4.3   Human-Machine Integration Constantly Developed in the Medical Metaverse

The medical field is suitable for the application of human-machine integration, and also promotes its further development. At present, human-machine integration has gone through two main stages in medical applications. The first stage is the traditional CAD computer-aided detection, which requires doctors to manually input images, extract features, classify, and then the computer will automatically output the results, which is inefficient and easy to "slip through the net". Based on this, the current human-computer integration has developed to the second stage, which not only creates a CAD technology based on deep learning, which is to build a deep, integrated network that simulates the human brain, automatically extracts essential features and outputs final results, and improves the accuracy of detection and diagnosis.

The rapid development of emerging technologies represented by information technology and artificial intelligence has greatly expanded the scope of time, space and people's cognition, and mankind is entering an era of intelligent interconnection of all things with the three-way integration of "human-machine-organism". As a typical scene in the era of "human-machine-organism" three-dimensional integration, medical and technology practitioners are further promoting the scientific theory, technical viewpoint and development system of virtual-real interaction, human-machine collaboration and the emergence of group wisdom, including Metaverse and human-computer integration, which will become an important carrier for accelerating the construction of a healthy China and realizing a healthy economy, and will also be the best testing ground for artificial intelligence technology.

5   The Natural Advantages of the Metaverse in the Medical Field

Metaverse provides a data basis for the comprehensive improvement of human health by comprehensively monitoring human microbiology, nutrition, psychology and other higher-level vital sign indicators, thereby finding biological targets for the health intervention, which is of vital importance to the development of the medical industry. The "Healthy China 2030 Planning Outline" proposes to comprehensively improve national health, which is consistent with the ultimate goal of the medical Metaverse to "cure the disease", so the Metaverse has a natural advantage in the medical field.

5.1   Visualize the Symptoms

CT, DR, MRI and all other imaging equipment, the goal is to visualize the disease, because the organ is inside the human body, is invisible, so the goal of the first generation of medical devices is to visualize what is invisible. For example, lung nodule localization and three-dimensional visualization technology, through medical devices to take out a piece of internal sliced images, so that "invisible" human organs "appear in their original form", and even build a holographic digital person, providing a reference for surgical planning.

5.2 Professional Doctor Widely Available

TeleMedicine and graded diagnosis and treatment can increase the inclusiveness of expert resources. For example, the First Affiliated Hospital of Zhengzhou University is known as the world's largest hospital, doctors are very tired and hard every day, how to extend the ability of doctors in large hospitals to the grassroots, which can use the power of new technologies such as Metaverse and AI to promote remote diagnosis and treatment, so that more patients do not have to go to the provincial city to see a doctor, get professional diagnosis and treatment at the doorstep of the family, and achieve "difficult empowerment, good and great".

5.3 Realize the Scenario of Psychological Diagnosis and Treatment

Most psychological problems actually stem from ineffective thinking, trapped in their own hypothetical situations and derived from stress. The general treatment method is similar to the case reorganization, allowing the patient to assume a situational role in the imagination, and the doctor guides the patient to make psychological relief. In the Metaverse, doctors can put the patient directly in it through virtual scenes, and the immersion and privacy of the Metaverse makes it easier for patients to focus, which can reduce the patient's failure to imagine or recall the past and other factors to affect the efficacy, while greatly shortening the time required for treatment. Virtual scenes can also create environmentally assistive therapies such as unethical, illegal or dangerous in real life. At the same time, psychological diagnosis and treatment in the Metaverse can break the cultural barriers and stigma labels between doctors and patients, so that patients can reduce their resistance to medical treatment, and it is easier to establish mutual relations with doctors.

5.4 Boost the Innovation of the Pension Model

With the arrival of China's retirement peak after 2022, the impact of the one-child policy over 30 years will make it difficult to continue the traditional pension model, both the country and the families will face the dual dilemma of pension.

Metaverse uses technologies such as speech recognition, intelligent control, interconnection of all things and virtual digital people to carry out old-age services, which will help solve the lack of energy and physical strength of the elderly people, ensure the safety of the elderly people at home, and reduce the occurrence of accidents; Big data technology produces digital identity numbers and identity QR codes for the elderly, combined with face recognition technology, to facilitate travel, medical treatment and social networking for the elderly; VR three-dimensional three-dimensional information service platform for the elderly, through the virtual scene method, so that the elderly can go shopping online without leaving home. Pension enterprises will fully present the service content in a virtual digital way, the elderly people can accurately choose the pension service that suits them through on-site immersive feelings. Platform pension enterprises are managed through the blockchain, open and transparent, to prevent the elderly from being deceived. Online work can support the secondary employment and entrepreneurship of the young and healthy elderly people, help to update their knowledge for free, let the elderly have something to do, the country, enterprises, individuals win-win.

6 Metaverse Application Scenarios in the Medical Industry

Based on the advantages of meta-universe medical applications, this paper believes that meta-universe medical application scenarios or paths mainly include and are not limited to the following aspects (Fig. 3).

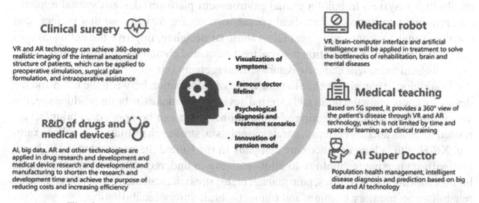

Fig. 3. Schematic of the medical application scenario of the Metaverse

6.1 Clinical Surgery

360-degree realistic imaging of patients' internal anatomy is realized through VR and AR technology, which is applied to preoperative simulation, surgical plan formulation, intraoperative assistance, etc. In the existing clinical surgical practice, there are problems such as the accuracy and safety of surgery, the limitation of medical surgical resources and poor communication between doctors and patients, etc. Metaverse element can be applied to the entire process from preoperative clinical surgery to intraoperative clinical surgery, through VR/AR, hologram and other technologies, to solve the difficulty of surgical lesion positioning, the shortage of medical surgical resources and poor communication between doctors and patients, etc. Its key application scenarios are reflected in the formulation of surgical plans and preoperative simulation, doctor-patient communication, intraoperative real-time imaging, intraoperative operation assistance and remote surgery.

For example, Vicarious Surgical's surgical machine in the United States can enter the abdominal cavity through a single incision of 1.5 cm or even smaller, providing a 360-degree full view, and the doctor obtains a panoramic sense of realism by wearing VR glasses and joysticks, as if entering the patient's abdominal cavity; Augmediics' Surgical Visualization AR system in Israel can provide doctors with "X-ray vision" in complex surgeries, indicating the location of surgical instruments in real time and correctly, allowing the surgeon to perform surgery even without looking at the monitor and without leaving the patient's eyes.

6.2 Medical Robots

VR, brain-computer interface, and artificial intelligence are applied to treatment to solve bottlenecks such as rehabilitation, brain and mental illness. The bottleneck of the existing brain and mental illness treatment is reflected in the lack of effective treatment of brain and nerve diseases, the clinical rehabilitation environment has limitations and other difficulties, and the application of medical robots, through the use of VR technology rehabilitation system to build a virtual environment platform, designs virtual rehabilitation training scenarios and medical operation tasks for patients, so that patients can use the virtual environment to generate a sense of presence, improve the enthusiasm of patients to invest in rehabilitation medical treatment, and combine rehabilitation training, psychological treatment and case database management into one.

In addition, it can also realize the exchange of information between the brain and the device by connecting the brain and external devices, and make the brain produce specific sensations through accurate current stimulation, which can be applied to brain/nerve-related diseases such as epilepsy, paralysis, aphasia, stroke rehabilitation, etc. For example, XR Health, a long distance care company in the United States, combines VR headsets with immersive technology to allow patients to undergo rehabilitation training at home, covering sports injuries, pain management, stress management, menopause, stroke rehabilitation, memory training, and traumatic brain injury rehabilitation.

6.3 Medical Teaching

Based on 5G speed, it provides a 360-degree view of the patient's disease through VR and AR technology, and is not limited by time and space for learning and clinical training. At present, there are pain points in medical teaching in terms of teaching scenarios are not realistic enough, medical anatomy physical specimen donors are insufficient, geography and case limitations, etc., Metaverse elements can be applied to enhance teaching of medical training, anatomy teaching and digital medicine library construction to solve the above problems.

For example, Oculus helmet technology is applied to the University of Connecticut Medical Center Plastic Surgery Residency Training, where doctors can see a series of surgical demonstrations in 3D images, have the opportunity to do it themselves, trial and error, and get immediate feedback from teachers; THE VR surgery training and simulation program provided by OSSO VR Company reproduces the operating room scene through highly realistic visual technology, allowing users to exercise the actual operation of various types of surgeries in a virtual environment through VR remote control devices; Allow surgeons to interact with new medical devices in a 3D space, increasing user familiarity with medical device companies' new solutions.

6.4 Drug and Medical Device Research and Development

AI, big data, AR and other technologies are applied to drug research and development and medical device research and development and manufacturing, shortening the research and development time and achieving the purpose of reducing costs and increasing efficiency. In the face of the current pain points in drug research and development and medical device development and manufacturing, Metaverse elements can solve the high cost of drug research and development, long research and development cycle, low success rate, and high precision requirements in medical device research and development.

For example, Exscientia has built three technology modules1 and formed a complete end-to-end AI solution from target selection to patient selection, with four major tasks: target selection, designing the right candidate molecules, collecting the right data, and selecting the right patients; Alva systems apply AR to medical device manufacturing, which can help realize the inspection of medical equipment production lines and equipment production lines, and realize the visualization of digital twin loT of production lines; Inspectors use a variety of mobile terminals such as AR glasses, mobile phones and tablets to three-dimensionally see the operating status and parameter values of the overall equipment, support gestures and voice commands to adjust the parameter display content, and greatly improve the inspection efficiency and accuracy.

6.5 AI Super Doctor

Based on big data and AI technology for population health management, intelligent diagnosis and prediction of diseases, AI super doctors can be applied to auxiliary diagnosis, health management and the disease prediction in view of the shortage of medical resources in China, the uneven level of medical technology and the pressure of cost control. For example, Evidation Health has teamed up with top pharmaceutical companies to advance exploratory research, such as Eli Lilly exploring the uses of smart device data to detect cognitive decline and mild Alzheimer's disease; 3-year collaboration with Sanofi to monitor daily living behaviors and health management for people with type ? diabetes; Qure.ai use deep learning technology to interpret medical images, screen for a variety of infectious and non-communicable diseases, and recommend personalized treatment options.

Although the development of the Metaverse is still in its infancy, it is expected to mature in the next decade with the cultivation of related technologies such as 5G, cloud computing, XR and ecosystems. At present, the application of Metaverse elements in various fields of health care has begun to take shape, and in the future, with the maturity of technology and capital investment, as well as the transformation of the normalization of the epidemic on the overall pattern of medical undertakings, the medical Metaverse will closely focus on the patient experience, actively innovate medical service content and service methods, establish an effective connection between reality and virtual integration, online and offline integration, and promote the realization of the grand vision of national health.

Acknowledgements. This research was supported by Research on the High Quality Development of Shenzhen Industrial System Under the New Development Pattern of Double Cycle (No. SZIIT2021SK010), Research on the Practice of Online and Offline Blended Teaching (No. SZIIT2021SK035), Research on the Influence Path and Action Mechanism of Enterprise Financialization on the Balanced Development of the Real Economy under the Background of Economic Uncertainty (No. SZIIT2022SK009).

References

1. Lening, G.: Value implications, innovation paths and governance frameworks of new consumption in Metaverse. E-Government (07), 30–41 (2022)
2. Ayun, Z., Bing, W., Min, X., Hui, L.: Application of metaverse in clinical teaching of surgery. Chinese Med. Educ. Technol. **36**(04), 390–395 (2022)
3. Xinshui, X.: The evolutionary process and growth dilemma of virtual digital man: an analysis of the "Dual Universe". Nanjing Soc. Sci. (06), 77–87+95 (2022)
4. Kaihong, W., Yuan, S.: A discussion on foreign metaverse research: hot spots, blockages and visions. J. Xinjiang Normal Univ. (Philos. Soc. Sc. Ed.) (05), 1–18 (2022)
5. Haiyang, Y, Lijun, Q., Tianxiang, J., Huili, J., Miao, Z.:Metaverse exploration and related suggestions. Internet Weekly (10), 45–47 (2022)
6. Shen, L., Jiangzhu, B.: A new trend in the development of "metaverse + psychology" integrating virtual reality. Psychol. Tech. Appl. **10**(01), 58–64 (2022)
7. Bob, W., Jia, L.: The best application of metaverse: medical exploration. Int. Brand Obs. (34), 38–39 (2021)
8. Jiang, W., Zhe, C., Pei, C., Chaocheng, H., Dan, K.: User information behavior under Metaverse Viewshed: framework and prospect. J. Inform. Resource Manage. **12**(01), 4–20 (2022)
9. Kaihong, W., Yuan, S.: A discussion on foreign Metaverse research: hot spots, blockages and visions. J. Xinjiang Normal Univ. (Philos. Soc. Sci. Edn.) (05), 1–18. https://doi.org/10.14100/j.cnki.65-1039/g4.20220602.001
10. Wei, Y., Xiannan, L., Lei, C., Yizhu, Z., Jun, W.: The operation mechanism, existing problems and suggestions for improvement of the "Internet+medical and health management" model. Mod. Hosp. **22**(05), 751–753 (2022)
11. Haotian, C., et al.: Analysis on the supply and demand of internet medical care in China under the COVID-19 epidemic. Health Vocational Educ. **40**(09), 136–139 (2022)
12. Liqing, L., Yulan, Z., Xiaoyi, H., Zuxun, L.: A study on the coupling and coordination relationship between primary medical resource allocation and economic development in China before and after the new medical reform. China Health Econ. **41**(05), 44–50 (2022)
13. Tao, L., Yue, Z., Ting, X., Lanqiu, L.: On the construction of online resolution mechanism for Internet medical disputes. Chinese Hospital **26**(05), 64–67 (2022). https://doi.org/10.19660/j.issn.1671-0592.2022.5.18
14. Yulou, J., Yicheng, Z.: The concept and application scenario of Metaverse: research and market. China Media Sci. Technol. **11**(01), 19–23 (2022). https://doi.org/10.19483/j.CNKI.11-4653/n.2022.01.004
15. Zhe, H.: Virtualization and Metaverse: the singularity and governance of the evolution of human civilization. E-Government (01), 41–53 (2022). 10. 16582/j.cnki.dzzw.2022.01.004

Cyberpunk and Cypherpunk: A Philosophical Analysis Comparing Two Views of the Metaverse

Ma Hanlin(✉) (iD)

Suzhou University of Science and Technology, Suzhou, China
fanfan2011cn2000@gmail.com

Abstract. As ancestors of the idea of the metaverse - Cyberpunks and Cypher-punks - propose two distinct attitudes towards Cyberspace, and this difference also infuses their attitudes towards the metaverse. These two attitudes will powerfully influence the developmental direction of the metaverse and how it will be recognized and accepted by society. Given that the visual space is an artificial reality created by technology, they not only illustrate two different ideas regarding "realities other than the physical one of human society", but also illustrate two different ideas regarding technology itself. The Cyberpunk view of the metaverse could be seen as techno-pessimistic or Luddiism. Cypherpunk's metaverse view, on the other hand, is "technological transformationism", which carries multi-possibilities of living styles of human being, and it almost incompatible with Luddism.

Keywords: Metaverse · Cyberpunk · Cypherpunk · Philosophy of technology

1 Introduction

The metaverse rose to prominence in 2021. It has become a pan-cultural phenomenon that sparks commentary and participation from a wide range of disciplines and industries. Corresponding to this is the uncertainty regarding its conceptual definition, technological standards, and evaluation methods. In other words, it is still difficult for us to get a precise unified consensus on the concept of the metaverse. Aside from the business and financial applications, I find two methods for evaluating the metaverse with partial consensus, which can be described as two views. Respectively, they correspond to virtual reality and internet technology with blockchain as the core. These two technological directions are also related to two similarly-pronounced concepts, namely "Cyberpunk" and "Cypherpunk". Historically, they have rarely been related to each other, and it is precisely the unified concept of the metaverse that has contributed to their rivalry.

The focus of this article is to analyze and compare views of metaverses from the perspectives of Cyberpunk and Cypherpunk. They happen to be related to two different attitudes toward the relationship between metaverse and the real world. The original ideal metaverse comes from Neil Stephen's cyberpunk novel "Snow Crash" [1]. These two attitudes will develop into different directions of investigation on the authenticity of "virtual cyberspace". When we examine whether the "virtual" should compromise with "reality", we will find that versions of the metaverse supported by different philosophical views of technology will take different paths.

© The Author(s), under exclusive license to Springer Nature Switzerland AG 2022
L.-J. Zhang (Ed.): METAVERSE 2022, LNCS 13737, pp. 81–91, 2022.
https://doi.org/10.1007/978-3-031-23518-4_7

2   Snow Crash and the Inappropriately Implemented Metaverse

Although there are different opinions on the technological standards and development direction of the metaverse, there is a consensus on the starting point of the concept itself. It originated in the novel "Snow Crash", and swept the world with Spielberg's film "Ready Player One", which duplicated the former's setting. For convenience of organisation, we will introduce the "metaverse" as imagined in "Snow Crash" as if divided into two parts: 1. The part which overlaps with the metaverse that has been realized or is expected to be realized currently; 2. The part that is different from the metaverse in the real world at the moment.

The concept of virtual reality (VR) was first proposed in "Snow Crash". However, the construction of the metaverse in our world requires not only VR technology but also a 3D modeling engine and a digital world physical construction system that can create a sense of "real" immersion. Although imperfect, these technologies have entered the stage of usability. Examples include the Oculus Quest 2, Unreal Engine 5, and the Omniverse virtual work platformare standouts in their respective fields. Based on the accumulation of technology, some companies with strong resources such as Meta (Facebook), Tencent, etc. have launched metaverse projects, which are committed to reconstructing the virtual environment for the office, education, social interaction, and entertainment.

In addition, the metaverse in "Snow Crash" is also a Sandbox game with a high degree of freedom, in which players can own and build virtual land and upload programs. In this game, metaverse regions would look very different due to the variety of tastes and technological abilities of players. A connected concept is User Generated Content (UGC). Namely, users create content, and the central platform only provides the basic framework. The "Warcraft map editor", and MOD production in "The Elder Scrolls" and "Mount and Blade" represent UGC. It is more thorough in "Second Life", Minecraft and Roblox with the independent production of virtual avatars by users of "Second Life" directly inheriting the story settings and plots in "Snow Crash". But these are not enough to construct a ideal metaverse, because users can not own their digital assets, without being manipulated by these companies.

The metaverse in "Snow Crash" is a highly decentralized network. There is no system administrator or backdoor system for manipulation, which means no super-system authority. It is a paradise for hackers and programmers. This makes it more like the Internet than a local system. Roblox and Sandbox which claim to be metaverse are not strictly decentralized enough (and Meta's Horizon Workroom is simply centralized). They may be metaverse-like in some respects, but the underlying technological logic has not yet reached the ideal standard. There are two reasons: 1. They have not been able to completely get rid of the traditional smart contract (computer program-based business or other human-machine/human interaction with value); 2. Some their network infrastructure (such as storage) is still centralized.

According to Nick Szabo (a cypherpunk) [2], traditional smart contracts (a centralized smart contract, such as a common buying and selling program on the vending machine) generally require a backdoor system. Such smart contracts require a "third party" to act as an intermediary to provide arbitration or deliberation for interactions between users in a system. Decentralized smart contracts need to be built on a public blockchain. Blockchain technology enables the confirmation of business communication interactions. It also enables part of the delivery work to be distributed to automated pro-grams based on hashing, signatures and specific consensus machnism of distributed pro-tocols. Ethereum is currently the most successful blockchain in the industry that deploys smart contracts. Developers build their smart contracts and decentralized applications on Ethereum through the Ethereum Virtual Machine.

But this is not enough. Although some metaverse projects like Sandbox are based on Ethereum in terms of value circulation and virtual property confirmation, ultimate control of the game operation is still in the hands of the developers. The real metaverse would never go offline and would have no access restrictions. At the same time, its software updates would not depend on any institution or individual and must be the result of the users' group resolution. It is difficult for commercial projects to include these characteristics.

Such a metaverse is a large decentralized virtual world, and building it requires upgrading of the internet infrastructure. For example, it requires the reconstruction of the underlying protocols of the Internet to establish a set of P2P storage protocols that can be used to distribute and store large-scale dynamic data. Projects such as the Inter-planetary File System (IPFS) and Arweave are working in this direction. Only when the decentralized infrastructure is completed will the metaverse – like the internet - never go offline.

From Meta to Tencent, from Roblox to Sandbox, the current metaverse projects on the market do not fully conform to the idea of the "Metaverse". They may have elements of it in some respects, but not enough for realizing the kind of metaverse imagined in Snow Crash. The two perspectives discussed in this article are related to this. Cyberpunk-style metaverse reviews, which focus on deviations of the metaverse from the reality of human society, often focus on the overlap of the current metaverse (VR technology) and that seen in Snow Crash; while Cypherpunk's expectations for the metaverse (an ultimate decentralized one) are based on the difference between it and the Snow Crash metaverse (they worry that its realizations are not decentralized enough).

3   Cyberpunk's Warning

From 2021 to the present, the metaverse has been reviewed endlessly. Most of these comments are related to keywords like "dystopia", "capital control", etc. These cyber-punk reviews warn of blind technological optimism and technological determinism, and also examine the negative effects of capital and power control in the process of social evolution brought about by technology. These dystopian stories take place in cyberspace. Among the classic movies, "Akira" (1998) directed by Katsuhiro Otomo, and "Ghost in the Shell "(1995) by Mamoru Oshii are typical cyberpunk arts.

The point about "immersive spaces built with virtual reality are not worth looking forward to" is one of the most frequent criticisms. The founder of the mobile game Poké-mon GO, John Hanke [3], wrote "The metaverse is a dystopian nightmare, Let's build a better reality". Commenting on the VR metaverse, he also said: What if technology could make us better? Could it nudge us to get off the couch and out for an evening stroll or a Saturday in the park? Could it draw us into public space and into contact with neighbors we might never have met? Could it give us a reason to call a friend, make plans with our families, or even discover brand-new friends? Collectively, could it help us discover the magic, history, and beauty hiding in plain sight?" Hanke's subtext is that the metaverse has taken us away from real life and reduced real human interpersonal-contact. We can see a similar warning in the film "Surrogates".

Hanke was just emphasizing the importance of the real world to human life, while another strand of cyberpunk metaverse commentary is more serious and philosophical. It review argues that the metaverse will pull humanity back into "Plato's cave" - into an inextricable fantasy. Philosopher Nozick constructed a thought experiment similar to the "Matrix" in his "Anarchy, State and Utopia" [4]: In it, people can knowingly choose to be in a container with electronic interfaces in their brains. By stimulating his brain, the best neuropsychologists provide him with whatever experience he desires. Nozick puts forward three reasons for rejecting the experience machine: 1. I want to do some (real) things, not just get the experience of doing these things; 2. For a person living in a container, there is no meaning in life, "it's the same as suicide"; 3. The experience machine cannot give the users anything more profound than the artificial virtual environment.

Nozick exhibits a social reality-centric approach, which we may call "physical reality-centrism". For him, the anchor point of value must be based on real society, and virtual reality is either "unreal" or just "second-class reality". The former heralds a kind of perception-centrism (such as Berkeley's "To exist is to be perceived"), while the latter still acknowledges the reality of the virtual environment, but does not value it. Neither of them expresses distrust of the maturity of the technology, but only of the technology itself.

However, perception-centrism is not suitable for providing a theoretical description of VR. David Chalmers [5] assumes that VR is an experience constructed by human perception. To him, human perceptions produced by VR are neither hallucination (generated purely by the human brain without external information input) nor illusion (with external – but misleading - information input).Crucially, in the VR environment, people only have a perception after receiving the information input, so it cannot be regarded as a hallucination.

Neither is VR perception an illusion. Chalmers uses an analogy to illustrate this: person (A) enters a restaurant and does not notice a large mirror in front of him. A perceives person B approaching rom the opposite direction, but in fact, B approaches from behind him. There are two conditions for this illusion. 1. A does not know that a device that does not reflect the "real" situation is inputting information to him; 2. A still cannot use this device proficiently. Just think about a rearview mirror. We know its existence and purpose, and we can use it skillfully. This situation is not an illusion. A person who has just entered the VR world is likely to have some illusions, which are the same as when we first watch a 3D movie. But if you become an "expert," you don't have this illusion and instead experience real interactions with others in this environment. All in all, it is hard to say that VR is an environment centered on constructing hallucinations and illusions.

Both Chalmers' "Digital Realism" [5] and Zhai Zhenming's "Perceptual Frame Equivalence Principle" [6] are trying to examine whether physical reality and virtual reality are equally real to human experience. In other words, they both see a virtual environment as a real scenario that provides causal interaction for humans. This response to Nozick is a reason for discounting his first objection. But his second objection must still be examined: can this virtual reality provide us with a meaningful life? Zhenming believes: "The difference of meaning is first related to the initial intention. This intention determines what kind of real changes the selected part (a constituent) of the object world should have (from the subject of intentional movement), and these changes does not reveal as the experience of human being, but rather the changes of realityy. The concept of success versus the concept of failure is originally about individual intentions, the concept of ownership is about the collective institutionalized intention of all individual participants, and the concept of moral responsibility is about the interaction between all individuals and the collective institutionalized intention " [6]. That is, as long as the actor can cause real objects to change in the VR world, this intentionality is real. Furthermore meaningful value concepts such as rights, success, and morality can be reduced to intentional relationships. Therefore, the VR world has the power to construct meaning.

In the end, only Nozick's third objection remains. Chalmers argues that this objection expresses a distrust of the artificial environment. But in this case, it shouldn't be just VR technology that is mistrusted: tech artifacts of the physical real world should not be trusted either. Chalmers appears to be suggesting a "Luddite" attitude towards VR technology (i.e. opposition to technological progress). The original Luddite workers who smashed machines were not opposed to all technology, but only the part of it that they could not adapt to. VR opponents don't have to reject all technological artificial environments, they just need to believe that the reality that VR constructs "doesn't feel right." They can indeed dentify many metaverse problems, such as "what if there is a bug in the system?"; "VR will cause dizziness, will it be harmful to the human body?"; "what if these technologies are used to control society?", and many more. However, it is theoretically consistent for them to be completely techno-pessimistic – because real-world technology also has negative effects on human society.

"Luddism" is different from outright techno-pessimism. The latter cannot theoretically reach a compromise with the metaverse, while the former can. Metaverse developers just need to develop some applications that don't make people uncomfortable. For example,as John Hanke said since human beings need a real-world communication environment, the metaverse might as well abandon VR and use Augmented Reality (AR), mixed reality (XR) and IoT technologies. However, will a metaverse that compromises with physical reality succeed? Holders of another view of the metaverse – the Cypherpunks – don't think so. In their view, cyberspace constructed by another important technology of the metaverse – internet technology – cannot compromise with the real world. Once humans try to do so, they are likely to get neither the benefits of the real world nor the benefits of the cyber world.

4   The Metaverse in the Eyes of Cypherpunk

The original "cypherpunks" were a group of privacy-protecting activists who emerged in the 1990s and advocated the idea of establishing the use of unregulated encryption technology in the United States [7]. Without such technologies there would be no contemporary-style internet or metaverse infrastructure. Blockchain, cryptocurrency technology, and the technological implementation of distributed systems have been influenced a lot by Cypherpunk and internet libertarian movements. In a narrow sense, Cypherpunks are cryptographers, engineers, and tech geeks who communicate with each other via email groups. The earliest Cypherpunk group was established in 1992 by Eric Hughes, Timothy C. May, and John Gilmore, and the name Cypherpunk was created by Jude Milton, inspired by the concept of "cyberpunk".

There are three notable concepts within early Cypherpunk: 1. The emphasis on privacy protection; 2. "Cypherpunk writes code"; and 3. The proposal of cryptocurrency. Eric Hughes states in the "Cypherpunk Manifesto" that privacy is different from secrecy. Privacy refers to information that the owner does not want the world to know (such as personal information), while secrecy refers to information that the owner does not want anyone else to know (such as a bank password). Privacy protection means that people can choose to expose only the necessary information (such as transaction information) in online interactions [8]. In the 1990s, there were no institutions in the United States that actively protected people's privacy, so Cypherpunks advocated the use of encryption technology, private mail, digital signatures, and encrypted currency to protect confidentiality by writing their own code and building open-source software. Hughes' understanding of privacy and how to protect it bodes well for the difference between the internet (the cyber world where the metaverse resides) and the real world. To be precise, what Cypherpunk maintains is precisely those characteristics of the internet that are different from the real world.

In addition, we need to think about what conclusions can be drawn when understanding regulatory issues in the context of this difference. "Cypherpunk writes code" shows an autonomous regulation scheme that is unique to the internet. At the same time, we also need to explore the technological philosophical presupposition behind it – the incorporation of value and technology, and cryptocurrency represented by Bitcoin is the concentrated expression of this view on technology.

Lawrence Lessig [9] stated that cyberspace is different from physical space, leading to the alienation of cyber legal regulation. These differences can be summarized in three points. 1. The inhabitants of the internet are born with the right to design code, which is similar to the ability to formulate the laws of nature in the real world. 2. The special "non-locality" in the online world does not directly correspond to the real world. 3. The concept of public and private in the online world is different from that in real society.

Firstly, let's look at an example from Lessig: the story of how "Dank's dog died after eating poisonous flower petals floating over from Martha's yard" [9]. Dank asks Martha to stop growing the plant, but the paradox is that if Martha stops growing the plant, she loses money, and it is her legal right to grow it in her yard. Dank says irrationally, "Why not make the petals poisonous only when in the possession of someone who has 'purchased' them? If they are stolen, or if they blow away, then let the petals lose their poison. But when kept by the owner of the plant, the petals keep their poison. Isn't that a solution to the problem that both of us face?".

The law naturally has a way to solve the problem between Martha and Dank in the real world, but it seems difficult to meet Martha's demands – which would mean eliminating the "negative externality". A world without negative externalities is full of readily available, economic "Pareto improvements", and cyberspace or the metaverse is thought to have the potential to become such a world. The owner of cyberspace is also the designer, and Dank can use coding to achieve Martha's request. He can even resurrect his virtual pet dog! Therefore, one observation we make here is that the ideal internet and Metaverse should have a different internal structure to the real world. The internet and the metaverse can provide people with an alternative way of life. But we must also be aware that codes can communicate regulations from physical reality, and humans can make cyberspace a space that resembles physical reality.

The second point is that the non-locality of cyberspace cannot correspond to real space. In the movie "The Matrix", there is a scene that illustrates this point: the protagonist opens any door to go to another location. This is an image metaphor for cyberspace. It seems that online residents can break the restrictions imposed by physical space on their network avatars. The transformation of life scenarios no longer requires commuting time, and people from different regions can meet in cyberspace easily at will. This asymmetry between the virtual and the real has led to many new phenomena. For example, human beings are moving into the era in which "close neighbors are inferior to netizens". And the more serious consequences come from the aspect of legal governance, Lessig gave this example of it [9]: In a country called "Boral", someone set up a gambling website, and law enforcement forced him to shut down the server in his country, but could not prevent the website from continuing to run and people continuing to visit it, because its servers could be set up in other countries. This is related to the non-local characteristics of the internet. When flipping between different life scenarios, netizens only need to change the information port without having to travel mountains and rivers to access the desired positions. To restrict a website, judicial authorities can order internet service providers to block the IP address of this website through legislation or administration. In this way, the non-locality of the network is artificially limited. For real laws to work in cyberspace, what they often need to do is not judicial work, but engineering and technological work in the name of justice—change the framework of cyberspace, and make it suitable for interaction with the physical world, and this means a centralized internet.

Thirdly, the regulation of cyberspace brings up some troubling situations. First and foremost are intellectual property and privacy issues. In Lessig's view, the purpose of traditional intellectual property law is different from the purpose of private law. Private property is exclusive: if someone else lives in your house, you can't live it yourself. Intellectual property rights are different. When others look at one of your paintings, it does not prevent you from also viewing the painting, and the dissemination of knowledge is beneficial to the production of knowledge. Therefore, the purpose of intellectual property law is to achieve a certain **balance** between the private rights of property owners, and the dissemination and re-creation of knowledge rather than to protect the permanent exclusivity of property rights. So Lessig said: " Intellectual property rights are a monopoly that the state gives to producers of intellectual property in exchange for their production of it. After a limited time, the product of their work becomes the public's to use as it wants. " [9].

This balance was easy to achieve before the creation of the internet because of the high cost of copying intellectual property. Nevertheless, in the internet era, the cost of copying information is extremely low, and the copying of information is a natural process of activity on the internet. This makes the protection of traditional intellectual property rights impossible to adapt to the Internet. The invalidation of the law has laid the way for people's creations on the Internet from elitism to populism. A culture called remix has arisen (which also prevails in the metaverse). There used to be a creative method called Anime Music Videos (AMWs), by which young people compile excerpts from anime and recomposed music to make videos. In 2015, Wind-up Records instructed an AMWs website to take down all films involving their intellectual property. The case was not legally complicated, but the question was how to completely remove any works related to remix culture. According to Lessig, the only way to fully achieve this is to have a "trust system" that monitors each hard drive for illegal data. The typical method is to store a program in the user's computer, and when it finds that the user has illegal information, it will call the police. But this upsets the balance between copyright holders' rights and free transmission of knowledge, and violates the privacy of users, putting them under the complete control of the Code Law.

The fundamental explanation for this is that the real-world "public-private" division doesn't seem to exist any more on the Internet. The judiciary either controls all networked computers through code (thinking that the Internet is a public domain) or completely ignores it (regarding that the Internet is a private domain). In a centralized Internet, businesses have other ways to protect intellectual property without resorting to overpowering "trust systems." They manage their resources through traditional smart contracts. For example, some movies can be watched for a fee on Youtube. Only when users pay and obtain an electronic certificate can they click to watch these videos. However, with the emergence of the P2P networks, these film and television resources can be obtained for free.

Another solution is Cohen's Law [9],which separates the network account from the real individual, and the network worm engaged in monitoring only knows that "14A" is watching, but does not know who is behind it. It also acknowledges that the web is a purely public sphere, and disconnected from reality. Even if Cohen's Law is used, to achieve intellectual property protection in a centralized network, it is necessary to obtain control over the user's local system and automatically delete or encrypt illegal files, which is not in line with Cypherpunk's demands.

Over the past 20 years, the internet seems to be gradually compromising with or follow the frame of the physical world. The right-to-code construction is gradually assigned to a few monopoly enterprises; the "localization" of the network is becoming more and more important, and users are gradually fixed in specific platform accounts and network areas. However, the "public-private boundary" in the network has never been effectively demarcated and regulated as in the real world (and rebuilding this demarcation seems to be a demand of the metaverse). These phenomena provide targets for the movement of Cypherpunks and their allies. From John Perry Barlow's (1996) "Declaration of Internet Independence" to Richard Stallman's "Free Software Movement", there is no shortage of claims that the rules of the Internet world are different and should not be the same as in the real world. In 2008, the Bitcoin system based on blockchain and cryptography, released by Satoshi Nakamoto, integrated almost all the ideas of internet independentists, which can be summarized as follows:

1. The concept of Cryptocurrency originated from Cypherpunk;
2. The Bitcoin system adopts the operation mode of free software [10], which was first uploaded to the open-source website SourceForge.net by Satoshi Nakamoto (later moved to Github), which is in line with the spirit of "Chpherpunk writing code";
3. Bitcoin is a p2p network that complies with Cohen's Law to a certain extent. The transaction data on its chain is public, but it does not correspond to actual personal identities, and it cannot be deleted. This is in line with the privacy-protection spirit of Cypherpunk;
4. The asymmetric encryption system in Bitcoin provides an innovative solution for "public-private division". The bookkeeper (or miner) in the public network can confirm the transaction, but cannot obtain control of the account. This right belongs only to the user who owns the private key;
5. The control right (accounting right) of the software is not concentrated in the hands of individual nodes, but is distributed in the hands of all those who obtain the right to produce blocks based on the protocol – based on the consensus machnism as proof of work. This is in line with the concept of decentralization of the Internet;
6. The software is a global network, like the internet and there is no access restriction. This is a characteristic of the famous "West Coast Code", which shows the non-locality of the internet;
7. The "double-spending" attack can be prevented through blockchain technology, thereby offsetting the challenge of "replicative features" to crypto currency, and at the same time, it does not use any real objects or imitated real centralized code identifiers as transaction tokens.

The relationship between Cypherpunk and the metaverse presents itself in two ways. First, the spirit of Cypherpunk and its allies is one of the consensuses among the builders of the metaverse. Secondly, various architectures created by Cypherpunks based on WEB3.0 technologies such as blockchain will become the infrastructure of the metaverse and will be gradually improved. Fred Ehrsam [11], the co-founder of cryptocurrency exchange Coinbase, wrote in 2017 that blockchain can confirm rights over virtual assets (such as avatars) in the metaverse. This is exactly the function of non-fungible tokens (NFTs). An NFT is a virtual token (essentially a smart contract) based on technological models (such as ERC 721, and ERC 1155) on a public chain such as Ethereum, which is non-replaceable data on the blockchain, can be used as a unique identifier, can be traded, and cannot be tampered with or deleted.

NFTs avoid the real world's reliance on physical objects and consensus to jointly confirm rights, and depends only on blockchain smart contracts and consensus. In addition to NFTs, blockchain-based currency provides an exclusive value token for the metaverse, and the development of decentralized finance, and cross-chain inter-operability also provides a foundation for the flow of value in different metaverse spaces. In addition to relying on blockchain, the current metaverse project also relies heavily on P2P protocol and the fact that internet residents can set up their own platform. At the same time it properly utilizes "replicability", a central feature of the internet. All of the above points to the difference between the metaverse and the real world. And this difference is created by Cypherpunk's successors in their contrivance of new technologies.

For Cypherpunks, cyberspace and the Metaverse may not be an ideal paradise. It is more like the rabbit hole in "Alice in Wonderland". It is full of risks, mistakes, and uncertainties, but it is also compelling, which makes people persistent in their exploration and invention. The adventurous nature of human beings constitutes the premise of this debate.

5   The Metaverse and the Philosophy of Technology

Whether or not to compromise with the physical world is only at the surface of a deeper debate about the nature of the metaverse. There are more profound philosophical explanations to be explored. Let's look at cyberpunk first. Nozick's views represent complete technological pessimism,which means technology iscapable of self-development: it has its internal developmental logic and is not dependent on human will. From this perspective, people would eventually become vassals of technology, just as people in the experience machine lose the sense of meaning in their existence.

Luddism seems to compatible with the existence of a technology-neutral theory. It means that technology does not necessary contain certain values. In the context of the virtual reality problem, the proposition becomes that the metaverse can follow the reality of the physical world. But technological pessimism and Luddism are not completely coincident, because physical reality no longer supplies the adaptive needs of all people.

Let's look at the philosophical perspective of Cypherpunk. Firstly, Cypherpunks are not techno-neutralists (or techno-optimists), because techno-neutralists believe that the ends and means of technology are only connected by chance. But Cypherpunks and their allies see the internet as a unique space of meaning and endow encryption with a purpose—to protect privacy. So they are not just using the internet and encryption as a tool. Secondly, Cypherpunks are not techno-pessimists either. The practical idea that "cypherpunks write code" is contradictory to the theory of technological autonomy. Then how should the Cypherpunks' view of technology be understood? The theories of " Transformation by Technology " may help explain (stems from the work of Wu Guosheng[12]). The so-called "transformation" here refers to activating the potentiality of reality, and transforming the philosopher Heidegger's "being" into "the thing of what it is". As "being", the way of life has the potential for innate difference and diversity. Technology is the process that makes this difference a reality. The internet created by Cypherpunk is a kind of "different existence" that is distinct from "real life" and experienced by a representative group of people who realize their lives through their specific technological means.

Technological transformationists will analyze various technologies specifically because different technologies reflect the demands of different groups of people. As a result, the development of a metaverse based on multiple technologies may be divided. But what is more worthy of our attention is whether "anti-technological" technology will appear in the metaverse, if the technology here means the initial way for carring multi-possibilities of living styles of human being. Before the advent of mechanized clocks, farmers' time were different due to different lifestyles: technology was determined by life. And the emergence of universal time in industrial society led to a uniformity of people's ways of life. The experience of human beings may be determined by industrial technology, but it has perhaps lost a certain type of "meaning". From this perspective, Cypherpunk's "entering the rabbit hole" may be counted as an effort to counter a certain uniformity through a different reality produced by different technological framework. The question of whether metaverse follows the domination by reality may be cast differently: whether humanity is compromising with the "anti-technology" philosophy of modern industrial society. Cyberpunks and Cypherpunks seem have distinct attitudes on this point.

6 Conclusion

We can now return to the core metaphor of Stephenson's "Snow Crash". The "Snow Crash" in the novel is essentially an information virus that can infect any information carrier, such as genes, languages (mind), or computer code. The infected system will enter a primitive state of disorientation. Language (and information technology) itself is a "technology" created for the "anti-Babel project", but it is not aimed at destroying the unity of mankind as in the Bible story, but to prevent mankind from returning to a primitive chaotic state and to provide a "vaccine" against the virus. Perhaps it is a coincidence that the "technology" discussed in this article should be the "transformer" that promotes diverse ways of life for human beings, rather than a provider of a uniform and empty "new order". With this understanding, we also have another interesting perspective to understand why internet geeks who advocate a metaverse model of "multiple" intercommunication do not like monopoly internet giants presenting their metaverse concepts to the market, even though such concepts may be acceptable to Luddites.

References

1. Stephenson, N.: Snow Crash: A Novel. Publisher, Spectra (2003)
2. Szabo, N.: Formalizing and securing relationships on public networks. First Monday **2**(9) (1997). http://firstmonday.org/htbin/cgiwrap/bin/ojs/index.php/fm/article/view/548
3. Hanke, J.: The metaverse is a dystopian nightmare. Let's Build a Better Reality. https://niantiI clabs.com/blog/real-world-Metaverse/. Last Accessed 10 Aug 2021
4. Nozick, R.: Anarchy, State and Utopia. Publisher, Basic books (1974)
5. Chalmers, D.J.: Reality+: Virtual Worlds and the Problems of Philosophy. Publisher, W. W. Norton (2022)
6. Zhengming: ZhaBetween Existence and Non-existence - a Philosophical Exploration of Virtual Reality. Publisher, Peking University Press (2007)
7. Jarvis, C.: Cypherpunk ideology: objectives, profiles, and influences (1992–1998). Internet Histories. **6**(3), 315–342 (2022)
8. Hughes, E.: A cypherpunk's manifesto. https://www.activism.net/cypherpunk/manifesto. html. Last Accessed 10 Dec 2022
9. Lessig, L.: Code: and Other Laws of Cyberspace. Publisher, Basic Books (2006)
10. Champagne, P.: The Book of Satoshi: The Collected Writings of Bitcoin Creator Satoshi Nakamoto. Publisher, e53 Publishing, LLC (2014)
11. Ehrsam, F.: VR is a killer app for blockchains. https://fehrsam.xyz/blog/vr-is-a-killer-app-for-blockchains. Last Accessed 2017
12. Guosheng,W.: Lectures on Philosophy of Technology. Publisher, Renmin University Press (2016)

Short Paper Track

The Application of the Metaverse in Ecological Education

Xuejiao Liu(✉)

School of Philosophy, The Institute of State Governance,
Huazhong University of Science and Technology, Wuhan 430074, China
hustlxj@163.com

Abstract. Ecological education is very practical in global ecological governance and ecological civilization construction. By creating a high‑fidelity environmental context, the metaverse ecological education is more likely to stimulate the ecological emotions of the learners, and then transform into a positive ecological behavior, which can effectively make up for the defects of traditional classroom ecological education. The metaverse ecological education is also facing new challenges such as digital monopoly, infringing learners' privacy, and learners addicted easily. Therefore, the meta-verse ecological education should adhere to the basic principles of people‑oriented, virtual and real balance, and sustainable. By improving teachers' digital literacy levels, creating a digital learning environment, it actively realizes the meta-verse ecological education. This is not only a realistic requirement for the construction of ecological civilization, but also a new topic facing the development of ecological education.

Keywords: Metaverse · Ecological education · Application

1 Introduction

In 1992, Neil Stephenson clearly proposed the "Metaverse" in the novel "Avalanche". It is exactly 30 years since the concept was first proposed. The concept of the metaverse has not yet formed an accurate and consistent definition. The word Metaverse is a portmanteau of the prefix "meta" and the suffix "verse". Thus it literally means a universe beyond the physical world [1]. Metaverse is a virtual space parallel to the real world and IS supported by AI, big data, HCI, and other communication technologies [2]. On October 28, 2021, Mark Elliot Zuckerberg, the founder of Facebook, announced that Facebook was renamed "Meta", and many media also called the "first year of the metaverse" in 2021. In many aspects of human world economy and life, it has become a key area for enterprises and government investment layouts.

The article first pointed out the important role of ecological education in ecological governance and ecological civilization construction, and then analyzed the theoretical feasibility and practical feasibility of the metaverse ecological education. Make up the defects of traditional classroom ecological education, so we should actively explore the feasible path of the metaverse ecological education. However, the metaverse ecological

© The Author(s), under exclusive license to Springer Nature Switzerland AG 2022
L.-J. Zhang (Ed.): METAVERSE 2022, LNCS 13737, pp. 95–102, 2022.
https://doi.org/10.1007/978-3-031-23518-4_8

education is also facing new challenges such as digital monopoly, infringing learners' privacy, and easy addiction. Therefore, on the basis of adhering to the basic principles of people - oriented, virtual reality, and sustainable, the digital learning environment and the development of application pilots to realize the metaverse ecological education, which is not only conducive to the construction of ecological civilization, but also has a profound impact on the development of ecological education in the future.

2 Necessity of Ecological Education

2.1 People Are More and More Concerned About the Quality of the Ecological Environment

The current ecological problems have become the key issues of human attention. Whether it is academic or practical practice, human research on ecological problems attaches great importance to. Because ecological problems itself has the characteristics of cross - boundary, complexity, and long - term nature, ecological problems have become a global issue at home and abroad, and ecological governance has become an important part of global governance. Nowadays, with the improvement of people's living conditions, the status of the ecological environment in the good life of the people is increasingly prominent. The high - quality ecological environment is closely linked to the happiness of the people, and the people's attention to the ecological environment is getting higher and higher.

In March 2022, Xinhua News Agency jointly released "Big Data to see the attention and expectations of the National Two National Sessions in 2022". The ecological civilization ranked fourth, and the construction of ecological civilization was still a hotspot of the whole people.

Many scholars have also carried out the study of the relationship between the ecological environment and the happiness of the people. Xu Zhihua [3] analyzed the effects of air pollution and water pollution on happiness by matching provincial pollution data and personal happiness data. The article shows that the increase in Nitrogen dioxide concentration and increased waste water discharge volume will significantly reduce personal happiness. Zheng Junjun [4] and other analysis of models and empirical analysis can be concluded that with the improvement of material living conditions, people's environmental protection concepts gradually enhance, and more actively pay more attention to and advocate green lifestyle. In the future the level of people's livelihood will be closely related to the quality of the environment. George Mackerron [5] use smartphones to conduct a questionnaire survey on more than 20,000 British participants. The type of green or outdoor activities is happier than in the urban environment, and the beautiful natural environment has a positive impact on personal happiness.

2.2 Ecological Education Helps Improve Environmental Quality

People have conducted research on ecological governance from all angles, such as putting forward different paths for ecological governance from the aspects of management, sociology, economics, political science, and philosophy. To realize the harmony between man and nature, it is not enough to rely on the efforts of experts and environmental protection departments and the improvement of policies and regulations. Ecological governance to concern everyone's interests requires the common participation of the general public. Extensive development of ecological education can effectively enhance people's ecological awareness, cultivate people's ecological consciousness, enhance people's ecological capabilities, and then effectively improve human ecological behavior. In the new era, in the face of new challenges, the new path of actively exploring ecological education is not only an effective way to solve ecological problems, but also a new issue facing ecological education.

The significance of ecological education is not just to increase the knowledge reserves of people's ecological environmental protection. The more important value of ecological education is to promote the change of human thinking concepts. The first is to change the value concept of human rule of nature in the past, and replace the values of harmony with nature and nature. Engels had warned, "Thus at every step we are reminded that we by no means rule over nature like a conqueror over a foreign people, like someone standing outside nature—but that we, with flesh, blood and brain, belong to nature, and exist in its midst" [6]. Ecological education makes people realize that the concept of conquered nature will eventually harm the interests of human beings and threatens human development, thereby transforming the binary concept of man and nature.

The second is to replace the world view of mechanical restoration theory that has been popular in modern times with overall ecological thinking. Through the study of ecological knowledge, people can scientifically understand the material and energy cycle of nature, deeply understand the whole and system of the ecosystem, and truly understand the importance of the balance between people and nature. Establish a scientific concept of "only one earth", man and nature are the community of destiny. The change of concept can effectively guide people to adhere to sustainable development consciously in life, practice green and environmentally friendly production, life, and consumption, and protect nature scientifically.

3   The Feasibility of the Metaverse Ecological Education

3.1   Theoretical Feasibility

The theoretical basis used in the field of ecological education is the development of Situated Cognition theory [7]. The Situated Cognition theory was formed in the mid -to -late 1980s and began to penetrate into the field of education in the 1990s. The Situated Cognition theory is that knowledge is born in the interaction between people and specific situations. "Knowledge is an activity, not a specific object; it is always based on the situation, not abstract; knowledge is constructed in the process of interaction with the environment, not objective decisions, nor subjective generated; Knowledge is a state of interaction rather than facts" [8]. Situation Cognitive theory emphasizes that situations are necessary conditions for learning and carried out. The situation has the function of clue guidance in students' learning activities, which helps students to retain the knowledge. In addition, the creation of the situation has achieved remarkable results in stimulating students' emotional experience and enhancing the effect of teaching.

The characteristics of the fusion of the metaverse can create the specific situation needed for ecological education under the support of technology. Metaverse created embodied social environment, based on block chain trust mechanism and high fidelity learning environment will effectively solve the problems of the learning space, such as learning environment distortion, centered on the student is difficult to realize, lack of learning immersion, and across time and space high-order thinking training, etc. [9] In the field of ecological education, specifically, traditional ecological education is limited by physical spaces such as school classrooms, which mainly depends on the instilling ecological knowledge, and emotional incentives are lacking. In addition, "environmental protection, ecological crisis and other behaviors have long feedback time and difficult to observe the results. It is difficult to link with the direct experience of the subject, and it is difficult to trigger an emotional learning mechanism" [10]. The high - fidelity learning environment created by the metaverse makes the content of ecological education more abundant and vivid, and the form of education is more diverse, which will stimulate the ecological emotions of learners. It can effectively make up for the defects of traditional ecological education. The metaverse is a new pattern, which is of great significance for improving the quality and efficiency of education and providing new motivation for the development of teaching and learning [2].

3.2 Reality Feasibility

Ecological education, as a powerful starting point for the construction of ecological civilization, has always been limited by the physical space such as school classroom, and mainly relies on the indoctrination of ecological knowledge. There are problems such as boring learning content and single form, which is not conducive to stimulating the ecological emotion of learners, and the effect of ecological education is not obvious. The outbreak of COVID-19 has shifted teaching from offline to online [11]. Many experts believe that this virtual universe has great potential in its application in education [12].

Some scholars have pointed out that with the help of embodied learning, the metaverse ecological education becomes easier to learn about environmental protection [13]. Due to the long - term and lagging of ecological consequences in real life, people often cannot feel the destruction of their own behavior on the ecological environment, and it is difficult to reverse the predicament of the ecological environmental protection. Education's immersive experience helps people intuitively feel the ecological consequences that cannot be experienced in real life. With the help of the physical environment implemented by the metaverse, the learning of the ecological environment has a positive role in stimulating the ecological emotions of learners, completely different from traditional knowledge - based ecological education, and has a positive impact on students' positive ecological behaviors. Education to create specific situations to stimulate ecological emotions through embodied learning, transform into specific ecological protection practice, and truly empower ecological education.

For example, the metaverse can be used to accelerate the degradation process of polyethylene plastic garbage in nature, so that people can intuitively feel the ecological consequences of plastic use and improper discarding, and greatly enhance people's emotional experience. The metaverse also can be used to realize the integration of ecological education and cultural tourism resources, and use the characteristics of the virtualization of the metaverse to allow learners to appreciate the magnificent natural scenery such as mountains, flowing water, ocean, and jungle, and stimulates students' love of nature. The integration of ecological education and historical disciplines helps learners travel to ancient cultural sites and comprehensively understand the relationship between man and nature. The immersive virtualization experience implemented by the metaverse is different from the simplicity of the pure knowledge teaching in the past. The metaverse can create an immersive learning opportunity to improve students' motivation for learning [14]. On the basis of learning the evolution of the relationship between people and nature, so as to promote the conscious environmental protection behavior of learners in reality and help the realization of environmental protection goals. Various forms of active interactions that occur in the virtual learning situation of the metaverse can become active information cognitive activities. This is more effective than passive knowledge learning [15].

4 The Way to Carry Out the Metaverse Ecological Education

4.1 What Problems Should Metaverse Ecological Education Pay Attention to

As the theoretical and technological development of the metaverse is still in the initial stage, the research of the metaverse is not yet mature. The introduction of the metaverse into ecological education requires as much as possible to avoid the risks and challenges that the metaverse may bring.

First, avoid new digital monopolies. The development of the metaverse needs to rely on high intelligent technology. It is difficult for ordinary users to occupy a dominant position in the digital age. It is impossible to master a large number of resources such as information and technology. Thousands of ordinary people are dominated easily by a few technology and capital giants. In the metaverse ecological education, we need to be alert to the monopoly and manipulated by companies with strong capital and minorities.

Second, pay attention to protecting the privacy of learners. The metaverse is considered a new form of the next generation of mobile Internet. It requires a large amount of data in the establishment and development of user identity and social relations. The data privacy and information security issues involved will be more complicated. If data security and privacy protection will be ignored, it will bring the chaos of the order of the metaverse, which will affect the relationship between people in the real world. "In the metaverse, the existing personal information and personal data protection laws and ethical specifications are far from this new trend" [16]. Actively improve the legal norms of personal privacy protection and data security. Pay attention to the privacy and security of individual users in the metaverse.

Third, avoid addiction and protect the physical health of learners. At present, the use of the metaverse needs to use specific tools such as VR glasses and helmets. If you use these devices for a long time, learners will have different degrees of physiological discomfort to endanger personal health. Some studies have reported that many children in the United States have symptoms such as nausea, dizziness, lost direction or loss of space consciousness after using VR helmets [17]. Therefore, the application of the metaverse ecological education will definitely adhere to the principle of moderate, restrict the use time of supporting equipment appropriately, and avoid the negative impact of the health of the metaverse ecological education on the health of the learner.

4.2 The Metaverse Ecological Education Should Adhere to a Few Basic Principles

First of all, metaverse ecological education should adhere to the principle of people-oriented and protecting reality. The educational metaverse should pay close attention to the actual needs of learners, and should not construct the educational content solely from the theory, and break away from the interests and needs of learners.

Secondly, the development of the metaverse virtual world should contribute to the realization of human happiness, and pay attention to the balance between virtual and reality. "The metaverse cannot replace the real world, but is a virtual digital space reflected by the real world, and cannot exist in isolation from the real world....It is the symbiosis, integration and co-creation with the real world" [18]. Although the metaverse has great potential in transforming human ecological education, it cannot completely replace the ecological education in reality. Metaverse ecological education is the extension of real ecological education, constantly enriching the content, way and form of ecological education. Exploring the new ecological education system of virtual and real integration is the direction of metaverse ecological education in the future, rather than replacing the reality with virtual. In essence, human beings always live in the real world, and the development goal of the metaverse should be to help human beings live better and happier in the real world.

Furthermore, metaverse ecological education itself needs to adhere to the principle of sustainable. "The metaverse has great dependence on virtual reality, data centers, data twins, etc., especially for network broadband, computing power, distributed storage, real - time touch interaction, cloud services, etc. The surge in power consumption needs to pay a large cost of environmental protection" [18]. The goal of the metaverse ecological education is to stimulate the ecological emotions of the learners, and then transform into positive ecological behaviors, and actively participate in the situation of improving the environment. If its own development is an activity that consumes resources, it will inevitably lose persuasion and is not conducive to the promotion in ecological education. Therefore, how to reduce the construction cost of the metaverse is also an important project that needs to be considered. The development of the metaverse cannot be separated from reality, and its construction must depend on reality resources. Therefore, it is necessary to consider environmental and resource constraints and adhere to the principle of green and sustainable development.

4.3 The Way to Promote the Metaverse Ecological Education

The realization of metaverse ecological education is a comprehensive project, which not only needs to pay attention to the digital literacy and ability of teachers, but also needs the efforts of the government, enterprises, schools and families, which is a systematic project.

The first is to improve the digital literacy and ability of teachers. The ecological education of the metaverse is different from traditional education. It can break through the time and space restrictions of the real world. It provides immersive learning through digital twin technology and continuously enriches the content and form of teaching. For example, to play the role of the metaverse ecological education in simulation of real learning situations, teachers are required to have the basic ability to build and apply scenarios [19]. How to efficiently integrate information about teaching content, student needs, spatial layout, and situation design, build more realistic teaching space, and correctly create a highly realistic situation such as historical scenes and geographical environment. The primary problem, actively carrying out diverse teachers' digital training, and striving to improve the digital literacy and ability of teachers is the prerequisite for the smooth progress of metaverse ecological education.

Second, multiple efforts are made to promote the practice of metaverse ecological education. The realization of the metaverse does not solely rely on the development of a certain technology, but needs to collect a variety of intelligent technologies, which has high technical requirements. Metaverse ecological education cannot be conducted without the support of intelligent technologies such as big data, artificial intelligence, Internet of Things, 5G/6G network, and also needs wearable technology devices such as VR glasses and helmets. To carry out the metaverse ecological education, we must improve the supporting technology and equipment, which is inseparable from the support of the government, enterprises, schools, families and other parties. For example, the government should support the development of relevant technologies, constantly improve the laws and regulations in the field of metaverse, and improve the normative system. Enterprises should continue to carry out technological innovation, use a variety of incentive to encourage the research and development of the metaverse technology, and provide technical support for the practice of the metaverse ecological education. Schools need to actively create a digital learning environment, and so on.

5 Conclusion

The metaverse has broad application prospects in the field of ecological education. The immersive experience achieved by digital twin and other technologies has unique advantages in stimulating learners' ecological emotions, helping to enrich the content and form of traditional ecological education, and optimize the actual effects of ecological education. It is of great significance to ecological governance and ecological civilization construction. However, because the development of the metaverse technology is still in its infancy, it is necessary to pay attention to the problems of the metaverse ecological education in digital monopoly and privacy. On the basis of adhering to the basic principles of people - oriented, virtual and reality, to improve teachers' digital literacy and abilities, the government, Enterprises, schools, and families have worked hard to promote the implementation of the practice of the metaverse ecological education, and give full play to the positive effects of the metaverse technology in the construction of ecological civilization.

References

1. Dionisio, J.D.N., et al.: 3D virtual worlds and the metaverse. ACM Comput. Surv. **45**(3), 1–38 (2013). https://doi.org/10.1145/2480741.2480751
2. Zhou, B.: Building a smart education ecosystem from a metaverse perspective. Mob. Inf. Syst. **2022**, 1–10 (2022). https://doi.org/10.1155/2022/1938329
3. Xu, Z.: Study on the influence and pricing of environmental pollution in the perspective of public happiness. J. Chongqing Univ. (Social Science Edition) **4**, 12–27 (2018). https://doi.org/10.11835/j.issn.1008-5831.2018.04.002
4. Zheng, J.: The impact of environmental pollution on happiness of Chinese. J. Wuhan Univ. (Philosophy Social Science Edition) **68**(4), 66–73 (2015). https://doi.org/10.14086/j.cnki.wujss.2015.04.009
5. Mackerron, G., Mourato, S.: Happiness is greater in natural environments. Glob. Environ. Chang. **23**(5), 992–1000 (2013). https://doi.org/10.1016/j.gloenvcha.2013.03.010
6. Karl, M., Frederick, E.: Marx and Engels Collected Works, vol. 25. Lawrence and Wishart Electric Book (2010)
7. Liu, J., Zhang, M., Wenfu'an: The educational value and theoretical foundation of the metaverse, education and equipment research (3), 6–11 (2022)
8. Xuhong, W.: Situation cognitive theory and its application in teaching. Contemp. Educ. Forum **10**, 9–10 (2008)
9. Li, H., Wang, W.: Metaverse + Education: a new state of educational development in the future. Modern and Long-distance Education (1), 47–56 (2022)
10. Liao, B., Zhang, X.Q.: Empirical research of operation mechanism ecological cognition on ecological behavior with mediators and moderators introduced. Resource Development and Market **34**(04), 539–546 (2018)
11. Li, H., Cui, C., Jiang, S.: Strategy for improving the football teaching quality by AI and Metaverse-empowered in mobile internet environment. Wireless Netw. (2022). https://doi.org/10.1007/s11276-022-03000-1
12. Contreras, G.S., González, A.H., Fernández, M.I.S., Martínez, C.B., Cepa, J., Escobar, Z.: The importance of the application of the metaverse in education. Mod. Appl. Sci. **16**(3), 34 (2022). https://doi.org/10.5539/mas.v16n3p34
13. Fu, W., Zhao, W., ZHuang, H.: An empirical study of the effectiveness of embodied learning in the edu-metaverse field. Open Educ. Res. **28**(02), 85–95 (2022)
14. Tlili, A., et al.: Is Metaverse in education a blessing or a curse: a combined content and bibliometric analysis. Smart Learn. Environ. **9**(1), 1–31 (2022). https://doi.org/10.1186/s40561-022-00205-x
15. Jaecheon, J., Soon, K.J: Explore educational use of Metaverse - based platforms. Korean Information Education Society Conference Book, Korea Information Education Society 361–368 (2021)
16. Weiwen, D.: Value anchor of metaverse governance: an investigation based on the relationship between technology and ethics. Governance **02**, 33–39 (2022). https://doi.org/10.16619/j.cnki.cn10-1264/d.2022.02.009
17. https://xw.qq.com/cmsid/20220415A097T900. Last Accessed 11 Aug 2022
18. Wang, Y., Wang, Y.Z., Wang, T., Jiang, S., Li, X.: The origin, development and educational implication of the metaverse. Chain Med. Educ. Technol. **36**(2), 121–129 (2022)
19. Xu, J., Wang, J., Zhong, Z., Zhang, G., Feng, S.: Challenges and measures of faculty development in the era of educational metaverse. Open Educ. Res. **28**(3),61–56 (2022)

Metaverse and Internet Youth in China

Kunjing Zhang(✉)

Shenzhen Institute of Information Technology, Guangdong 518172, People's Republic of China
2013100916@sziit.edu.cn

Abstract. The rapid development of the Metaverse will certainly affect the work, study and life of internet youth in China. The cause and purpose of this paper is make the Metaverse better serve the growth of internet youth in China, so that the Metaverse can not only meet their personalized needs, but also can guide them to make a contribution to the modern powerful country. In order to make internet youth in China make more outstanding contributions to the country's prosperity and prosperity on the new journey of building a modern socialist power in the future, China's educational circle needs to embrace the arrival of the Metaverse era in a positive way and use the most advanced information technology to realize the revolution of learning. To stimulate excellent character of the young generation in which innovation, creation, entrepreneurial ability and love for the motherland.

Keywords: Metaverse · New Generation of Chinese Internet · Internet youth · Online education · Education technology

1 Introduction

The rapid development of the Metaverse will certainly affect the work, study and life of internet youth in China. How to make the Metaverse better serve the growth of internet youth in China, so that the Metaverse can not only meet their personalized needs, And can guide them to make a contribution to the socialist modern power is the cause and purpose of this paper.

Historical Background of this Research: The future is here. The Metaverse, which used to appear only in science fiction and movies, has gradually become a reality and will have a profound impact on the future development of Chinese and even the world's youth. The year 2021 is known as the first year of the Metaverse because of the listing of Roblox, an American online game and social platform company, on the New York Stock Exchange, and the name change of Facebook, an American Internet giant, to Meta. It has also attracted many investors to flock to this field. The speculation with capital is believed to accelerate the integration of the Metaverse with reality and enter the life of the public. The concept of the Metaverse originated from the concept mentioned in Snow Crash, a science fiction novel published by the American novelist Neil Stephenson in 1992. It is a highly interconnected universe with virtual reality. At present academia for Metaverse is no authoritative definition.

© The Author(s), under exclusive license to Springer Nature Switzerland AG 2022
L.-J. Zhang (Ed.): METAVERSE 2022, LNCS 13737, pp. 103–110, 2022.
https://doi.org/10.1007/978-3-031-23518-4_9

Metaverse is based on the artificial intelligence, virtual reality, augmented reality, blockchain, brain machine interface, sensors, 5G network integration of modern information technologies such as digital ecosystem, it can provide users with immersive experience, to create a decentralized social space. We can feel the application scenarios of the Metaverse in movies, novels and games such as "Avatar", "Ready Player One", "Real Name", "Minecraft" and "The Matrix".

Current Situation and Trends of this Research at Home and Abroad: "Digital virtual space has changed the traditional definition and structure of virtual community. The author mainly studies the virtual learning community and virtual practice community. The author points out that the communication of the virtual learning community includes the sharing of knowledge, experience, ideas and information, and the members of the community produce knowledge through collaboration. The exchange of virtual Community of practice is the sharing of practical experience and working methods among the members of the community. The author further defines the virtual learning community of practice, that is, the interaction of reading, discussion and reflection among the members of the community has changed the traditional learning and practice ways. So digital virtual environments can create a real virtual world [1]." "The Metaverse is a computer-generated world in which the prefix" Meta- "refers to transcendence in a way that differs from metaphysical transcendence. It refers to a fully immersive 3D digital environment or "shared online space". "The Metaverse is made possible by immersive realism, ubiquitous access and identity, interoperability, and scalability." [2] "The use of new technology devices, such as head-mounted displays, supports the unification of real and virtual Spaces, thus creating a space for the fusion of virtual and augmented reality in the Metaverse. This service is called 'Metaverse exhibition experiential content service'." [3] "This paper discusses three possible harms or inequalities brought by virtual reality technology to society. The author believes that people have not formed effective prevention and governance mechanisms for these problems." [4] "Taking the quantitative characteristics of digital technology as a clue, it reveals that digital technology has a ubiquitous and pervasive character in dominating individuals. The author believes that digital media and the ideological discourse behind it have played a role in the standardization and even disciplining of the individual society." [5] "The Internet youth in China has profoundly influenced the change of Internet social mentality in terms of social issues, social emotions and social values. Behind it is the unique spiritual needs and characteristics of Internet expression of this group. According to the life development cycle and pressure of the new generation of the Internet, the state and society should promote the construction of richer, more diverse spiritual and cultural products with more political aesthetic characteristics of the new generation. At the same time, we should fully trust and understand this generation, stimulate the new generation's sense of political status, and enhance the new generation's political discourse power. Provide a more adequate expression platform and participation space through appropriate means to enhance their political sense of achievement; It is the core issue of whether the mainstream ideology can effectively guide the new generation of the Internet to make people younger simultaneously in multiple dimensions such as the construction of communication content, communication platform and communication channel." [6]

This research is very important for the healthy development of the Internet youth in China in China. With the increasing popularity of the Metaverse, China should pay more attention to how to guide the new generation of Chinese network to better adapt to the development mode of the future digital ecology, which will help the new generation of Chinese network to grow up and adapt to the development needs of the country. The new generation of Chinese Internet is the main force of modern socialist power. The research significance of this topic is to make them better embrace and adapt to the Metaverse, in which they can not only realize their life value but also make more outstanding contributions to national prosperity and rejuvenation.

2 Methods

This topic adopts the literature research method. At first, by Metaverse related literature collection and research, to understand the Metaverse in the field of education at home and abroad about Metaverse application of relevant research results. At second, combined with the feature of China's Internet generation of youth and the data of the related research achievements of theory and practice of research and analysis. At last, the paper tentatively puts forward how to better application Metaverse to education guide Chinese youth positive, contribute to the prosperity and strength of the country.

3 Results and Discussion

3.1 The Metaverse will become the Mainstream Development Model of Digital Ecology in the Future

In 2021, the US tech giants began using the Metaverse to describe the future of the Internet and digital ecosystem. They believe that the Metaverse is a super complex, which integrates digital twin technology, brain-computer interface technology, robotics, artificial intelligence, cloud computing, blockchain and other cutting-edge technologies, and then integrates into a complete ecological closed-loop. At present, the application scenarios of the Metaverse are successively in the fields of online games, social networks, e-commerce, digital education and so on. It is believed that with the development trend of the Metaverse technology, it will cover the whole real life scene.The digital ecology of the Metaverse is characterized by the following four points.

(1) Incorporate Reality

The biggest feature of the Metaverse is the fusion of virtuality and reality. It can virtualize all real scenes through digital twin technology, allowing users to experience different scenes and lives through digital people traveling through time and space. Virtual reality and augmented reality technology can also be used to traverse into real life, communicate and work with real people, giving users a sense of complete immersion experience.

(2) Decentralize

We know that in today's Internet world there are central servers, like the United States they are the center of the Internet, they developed the Internet and they dominate the core technology of the Internet. But in the Metaverse, which is a decentralized virtual world, there is no absolute authority that can influence this world." The concept of 'decentralization' is closely related to the blockchain, which is the fundamental feature of the blockchain system. The blockchain system is a point-to-point system where every node is equal and there is no centralized controller of the system." [7]

(3) Enhance Virtual Social Interaction

Based on Internet technology, people have realized the virtual social, enlarged the scope of social, but based on the Metaverse virtual social will have more reality, accompanied by the use of high-tech apparel technology, users can not only hear see more able to feel the real touch and smell, it is also motivate people into yuan virtual social universe is yearning.

(4) Keep Evolving

The greater charm of the Metaverse is that it will continue to evolve, and with the in-depth application of cutting-edge information technologies such as artificial intelligence, it will accelerate the upgrading of the existing Metaverse. Finally, it will realize the deep integration of people, society and digital, and create an infinitely expanding virtual world.

3.2   Internet Youth in China

Internet youth in China refers to the young people born after 1990 and 2000, who grew up with the Internet, are very skilled in the use of Internet applications, and have certain social dependence on the Internet. "The Internet youth in China is driving the generational change of values in Chinese society." [6] The growth of the Internet youth in China is accompanied by the rapid development of China's reform and opening up, and their growth environment has changed greatly from that of their parents. With the help of Internet information technology, they are more likely to accept new things, and their social mentality also has significant characteristics of the network era.Specific performance for the following aspects:

(1) Advocating Individual Freedom

The Internet youth in China pursues personal freedom and likes to live an unfettered life on the Internet, which has the characteristics of decentralization. The Social Governance Research Center of Fudan University conducted a survey on the mentality of college students in 2016 and found that 42. 1 percent of college students advocated personal freedom first. In real life, the younger generation is also self- centered, not caring about other people's feelings, only care about their own preferences.

(2) Want to be an Internet Celebrity

Internet celebrities are a special group in the Internet age. They have realized many young people's dream of becoming rich through the Internet. The network broadcast has brought a lot of goods, so that ordinary young people can realize their dream of becoming rich overnight, and make money through the network day by day. However, this group of young people is only a minority group among a large number of Internet users, most of whom are just ordinary Internet users. However, this phenomenon also shows the resistance of the young generation to the real life. It is difficult to realize the dream of becoming rich overnight in the real world, but the Internet provides them with the possibility.

(3) Pursuing Globalization

The new generation of Chinese Internet, pursuing globalization, is not satisfied with the use and access rights of the existing Internet in China. The Internet has provided the young generation with the possibility and way to embrace the world. For the sake of national security, China's Internet does not have complete access to the world's Internet. For example, young netizens cannot directly access Facebook through the Internet. But for the Internet youth in China, because they pursue globalization, some young people meet their Internet needs through VPN. According to a 2019 survey conducted by the Center for Communication and National Governance Studies of Fudan University and Zhejiang University of Media and Communication, 47.3% of college students have used foreign brands to expand their social circle, 39.8% have used the wall to watch short videos and TV dramas, and 15.9% have used the wall to obtain learning resources.

(4) Formation of Circle Network

With the growth of the new generation of the Internet, the pressure is gradually increasing. In order to release pressure, some interest groups are gradually formed on the Internet, such as "kua group" and "dui group", which attract a large number of young people to participate. Through the communication and interaction in the social circle of this subculture, young people have a strong sense of belonging and identity, which is the typical characteristics of the network circle. The main reason for the formation of this kind of circle network is that the pressure of young people in real life can not be well released, so they seek for a comfortable and mental balance in the virtual world.

(5) Having Strong Positive Political Emotion

The Internet youth in China pay more attention to the discussion of China's political issues, and all show a positive emotional orientation. For example, they pay more attention to topics such as "reform and opening up", "Belt and Road", "National Day" and "poverty alleviation", and are willing to express their positive feelings towards the country through their own discourse system. For some "insult to China" topic, the Internet youth in China also showed strong negative feelings. Through the positive and negative data comparison of the network new ecology has strong positive political emotion, love their own country.

3.3   How to Make Metaverse Help the New Generation of the Internet Grow?

The Metaverse can do everything the new generation of the Internet wants, allowing them to enjoy the freedom of life in the virtual world, to become Internet celebrities, to have unlimited access to the world, to form their own network of circles, to express their political feelings. But in the future digital ecosystem, how to let internet youth in China thrive is a problem that both the education and technology sectors should pay attention to. In the outbreak of the new champions league, against the background of more and more youth are accustomed to online education, after a period of study also revealed the weaknesses and disadvantages of online education, for example, when the teacher online delivery due to the poor students' learning self-control, class students listen to the teacher not online state, but rather on the network, is in bed, watching movies, playing games and so on. There are some young primary school students because of online classes caused by the decline of eyesight, also caused a lot of parents' anxiety, etc., similar to the problems caused by online education, and these problems are directly related to the quality of online education, so it is urgent to solve. The popularization and application of the Metaverse will help to combine the characteristics of the new generation of network, create a new online education model to give students immersive experience, overcome the drawbacks of previous online education, improve teaching quality, and make the new generation of network grow better. Specifically, the following ways can be used to solve the problem.

(1) Use Virtual Human Technology to Realize Multi-Scene Learning

In the Metaverse, the new generation of network can use virtual human technology to completely immerse in the virtual simulation classroom, face to face with classmates and teachers, your every move will be real, real-time display in front of everyone, to achieve a completely normal communication. It is no longer a simple online way such as virtual avatars, which also avoids the phenomenon of detachment from the teaching scene in the past online education. It not only realizes the effective transfer of knowledge, but also satisfies the social psychology of young people and contributes to healthy growth. In addition, the new generation of network can also make full use of the world's high-quality education resources, join different study groups, communicate and learn, realize the perfect leapfrog of traditional education, and avoid the drawbacks of the current general sense of online education, which will also cause the future learning revolution.

(2) Create an Empathic Experience Using Immersive Interaction Technology

In the general sense of online education, if the teacher wants to let the students feel the scene of the present, future and history, the most is to give students a relatively intuitive learning experience through the form of videos and movies. But in the Metaverse, you can recreate the scene completely, and the Internet generation can not only travel to the Cretaceous dinosaur world to explore the mystery of dinosaur extinction; They can also go to other planets in the future for scientific research exploration and learning. This kind of time and space shuttling will give young students more shocking learning experience, give students more rich learning feelings, and help improve the quality of education.For example, the education of ideals and beliefs. Usually, the teacher will explain to the students the good character of outstanding people and their suffering life experience, through the form of stories and videos to let the students feel the importance of ideals and beliefs. With the aid of the virtual space of the Metaverse, can let all revolutionary figures life experiences in virtual scene, let the student through the virtual "I" feeling to complete the fine qualities of the excellent characters is how to form, to give them to touch the depths of the soul, inspire young students set up the lofty ideal faith, efforts to learn from the excellent model and emulate.

(3) Use Digital Twin Technology to Carry out Simulation Practice

The use of digital twin technology will be able to create a virtual world completely parallel to the physical world symbiosis, so as to realize the reconstruction of virtual identity in the meta-universe, so that "self" can realize the value of life in the virtual world. For example, to let young students cherish peace and reject war. Students can participate in a "real" war in the virtual world, so that they can feel the horror of war and the fragility of life, so that they can feel that peace in the real world is hard to come by, so that they can make their own contribution to peace in both worlds. Through the digital twin "self", we can realize the practice of various scenes in real teaching without worrying about causing economic loss and life injury. This practical teaching mode is of great help to improve the innovation and creation ability of young students.

(4) Use Blockchain Technology to Improve Security Protection

The Internet is not a lawless land, and the same is true of the Metaverse. In order to effectively avoid the "decentralization" of the Metaverse, all data can be tracked through blockchain technology, so as to protect the privacy and personal and property security of the new generation of the network. In the Metaverse world, everyone can become any self you want, which is easy to produce dangers that cannot be anticipated and controlled in real life. Using blockchain technology, people who want to do whatever they want in the virtual world can be warned and let them have scruples. The Metaverse is not a place outside the law, technology is a place that can contain those who have evil ideas.

4 Conclusion

In order to make internet youth in China make more outstanding contributions to the country's prosperity and prosperity on the new journey of building a modern socialist power in the future, China's educational circle needs to embrace the arrival of the Metaverse era in a positive way and use the most advanced information technology to realize the revolution of learning. To stimulate the young generation of innovation, creation, entrepreneurial ability and love for the motherland excellent character. We have every reason to believe that the Metaverse will give the Internet youth in China more space for development and more opportunities to realize their life dreams. Let the whole world unite together to create a Metaverse belonging to the people of the whole world, so that more educational opportunities can be presented to every young person more fairly, and give them a better future. This is also the perfect embodiment the concept of "Community of human destiny" advocated by China.

Acknowledgements. This research was supported by 2021 Guangdong Provincial Youth Research Project: Research on the value goal and path innovation of young Marxists in the new era (No. 2021GJ047).

References

1. Moretti, G., Schlemmer, E.: Virtual learning communities of practice in metaverse. Virtual worlds and metaverse platforms: new communication and identity paradigms (2012)
2. Dionisio, J.D.N., III, W.G.B., Gilbert, R.: 3D Virtual worlds and the metaverse: current status and future possibilities. ACM Comput. Surv. **45**(3), 34 (2013)
3. Choi, H., Kim, S.: A content service deployment plan for metaverse museum exhibitions: centering on the combination of Beacons and HMDs. Int. J. Inform. Manage. **37**(1), 1519–1527 (2017)

4. Egliston, B., Carter, M.: Oculus imaginaries: the promises and perils of Facebook's virtual reality. New. Media Soc. 24(1), 70–89 (2020)
5. Kim, J.: Algorithmic intimacy, prosthetic memory, and gamification in black mirror. J. Popular Film Telev. **49**(2), 109–118 (2021)
6. Zheng, W., Yue, Y., Yong, G.: The new generation of network and the mentality of network society: generational change, mentality change and guidance path. J. Youth Explor. (2) (2022)
7. Li, Z.: Will the Metaverse become the mainstream development model of digital ecology in the future? J. World Knowl. (7) (2022)

The Research of Metaverse Application in Intelligent Railway Passenger Station

Xiaoshu Wang[1](✉) 🄳, Tianyun Shi[2], Wei Bai[3,4], Kaibei Peng[3], Jun Li[3,4], and Yajing Shi[3,4]

[1] Postgraduate Department, China Academy of Railway Sciences, Beijing 100081, China
xs6wang@126.com

[2] Department of Science, Technology and Information Technology, China Academy of Railway Sciences Corporation Limited, Beijing 100081, China

[3] Institute of Computing Technology, China Academy of Railway Sciences Corporation Limited, Beijing 100081, China

[4] Beijing Jingwei Information Technology Corporation Limited, Beijing 100081, China

Abstract. As an emerging concept, the metaverse has received a lot of attention and is now being researched for applications in many fields, including industry, education, healthcare, cultural tourism, and the construction industry. An enhanced intelligent passenger station architecture is proposed in China for railway passenger stations, which promoting the development of the metaverse application in Intelligent Railway Passenger Station (IRPS). To provide a theoretical support for the development of metaverse application in IRPS, the technology architecture of the metaverse railway intelligent passenger station is proposed, and the metaverse application in IRPS is designed, which lays the cornerstone for further intelligent development of China's high-speed railway.

Keywords: Metaverse · Intelligent railway passenger station · Intelligent railway · Application design

1 Introduction

In the novel 'Snow Crash' [1], the Metaverse concept was first proposed, which is a parallel world in information space aligned with real space. In the Metaverse, people build their playmaker, Avatar, that creates value that can circulate in the real world. In recent years, the COVID-19 pandemic has enormously impacted people's lives, and the metaverse makes it possible to solve the problem. For the features of the Metaverse, such as permeation, interactivity, anytime, anywhere, low latency features, and so on. It enhances the traditional industries' evolution. In this paper, based on the previous studies of Intelligent Railway Passenger Station (IRPS), the technology architecture of the Metaverse in IRPS is proposed. The metaverse application in IRPS is designed to promote the intellectual development of IRPS in information space that extends the temporal and spatial scale of Intelligent Railway.

The Metaverse is a technology gathering that includes 5G communications, cloud computing, digital twins, artificial intelligence (AI), blockchain, and expanded reality

© The Author(s), under exclusive license to Springer Nature Switzerland AG 2022
L.-J. Zhang (Ed.): METAVERSE 2022, LNCS 13737, pp. 111–117, 2022.
https://doi.org/10.1007/978-3-031-23518-4_10

technologies [2, 3]. The signature of the metaverse is immersion, interactivity, anytime, anywhere, and low latency. A virtual environment of the metaverse based on the actual physical world that incorporates real-world economic, social, and entertainment activities and allows for multi-user participation in its creation [4].

The Metaverse advances industrial automation [5]. BMW is building a virtual factory with Omniverse to pre-build digital models before building cars. Production efficiency by about 30% [2].

The combination of metaverse and education [6] can enhance physical practices in the schooling process, improve the efficiency of participatory activities, enhance daily sensory experiences, and provide technical support for the construction of virtual learning communities, gamification, and personalization of teaching and learning, contributing to revolutionary changes in education.

Metaverse is exploring applications in the medical field [7], emerging in several aspects of medical prevention, diagnosis, treatment, and medical education. The health metaverse is one of the innovative solutions to address the global healthcare challenges that usher in a profound digital transformation of the worldwide healthcare system.

Metaverse is highly consistent with the genes of cultural tourism activities, cultural tourism development needs, and development paths [8]. During the COVID-19 pandemic, the metaverse will promote the development of film and animation, game experience and interaction, performing arts content and presentation effects, digital operation of large festivals and exhibitions, protection of cultural and tourism resources, intelligent tourism, and other aspects.

The potential application scenarios of a metaverse in the construction field [2]. In the design stage, the metaverse can provide a space for communication in the virtual world, build a virtual design plan model, and break through the space limitation of communication; in the construction stage, preview the construction process and complete the verification and adjustment of complex engineering construction plans; in the operation and maintenance stage, use the metaverse virtual space to expand the functions and operation and maintenance; and conduct virtual construction transactions in the virtual area.

Even though the metaverse application is exploratory, the current research results show that the metaverse technology can promote the progress of many fields. The metaverse technology lowers the cost, promotes efficiency and precision rate, expands the spatial scale for many domains, and provides interaction beyond time and space. With the development and maturity of metaverse technology, it is bound to carry a new qualitative leap in many fields.

2   The Technology Architecture for the Metaverse of IRPS

In China, the IRPS concept was first proposed in 2017. Meantime, the "1 + 4 + N" master plan was constructed [9], where "1" means a brain, "4" includes passenger service, station management, safety, and green, and "N" means numerous applications in the railway station. Development until 2021, the concept of an enhanced intelligent railway passenger station was proposed by the continuous research of cyber-physical and digital twin technologies in IRPS. The Enhanced IRPS realizes the convenient travel of passengers [10], Seamless self-service, an efficient organization of production, secure real-time monitoring, green and eco-friendly, through building the fully interconnected physical station and fully mirrored digital twin station for physical-information mapping fusion, total sense simulation, real-time monitoring, precise diagnosis, deducing the state of a predicted physical entity in a real-world environment. The analytics platform layer of The Enhanced IRPS's overall architecture compose by the platforms of data aggregation and sharing, controlling and collaboration linkage, intelligent service, cloud computing, digital twins, internet of things, big data analysis, and other platforms.

The metaverse incorporates various new information technologies such as 5G communications, edge computing, digital twins, artificial intelligence, blockchain, and virtual/augmented reality [11]. The metaverse forms a virtual world in information space that is identical and independent of the real world [4]. The railway metaverse covers the entire society-physics- cyberspace of railway transport and makes rail transport transcends the limits of time and space, which advances the opening of the railway with additional socioeconomic advantages.

The basis on the platform of the enhanced IRPS, Metaverse technology can be realized in railway passenger stations, and The Technology Architecture for the Metaverse of IRPS is as follows (Fig. 1).

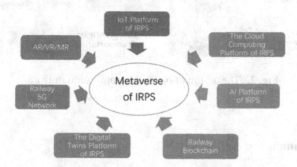

Fig. 1. The technology architecture for the metaverse of IRPS

The IoT platform of IRPS collects information from the real world, which supports connecting the virtual world IRPS and the real world IRPS. The cloud computing platform of IRPS provides powerful computing capabilities, which make the end devices lighter. The AI Platform of IRPS includes big data analysis and AI algorithms, which determine the metaverse application in IRPS and how smart it is. The Railway blockchain supports the metaverse application in IRPS economic system, ensuring the safety of the virtual identity and assets of metaverse users and ensuring the legitimacy of transactions. The digital twins Platform of IRPS establishes a digital mirror of some railway station, realizes the full mirror of the real world to the virtual world, and provides a basis for the virtual primary metaverse, the virtual-real symbiosis, and the virtual-real linkage of the railway intelligent passenger station. The Railway 5G Network is a channel for the metaverse to provide low-latency, high-speed, and large-scale access, providing users with a more real-time and smooth experience. AR/VR/MR technology offers an immersive metaverse experience, allowing users such as travelers and staff to interact with virtual objects.

3 The Design of Metaverse Application in IRPS

Many digital twin stations have been preliminarily constructed in IRPS. On this basis, the application of the metaverse in IRPS is designed, including Virtual Humans, passenger service, passenger transportation, Safety &emergency response, energy management, comprehensive transportation hub, and so on (Fig. 2).

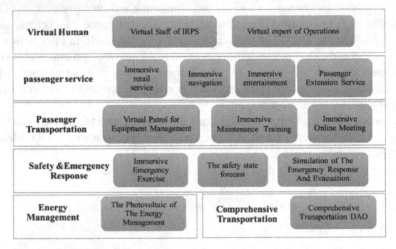

Fig. 2. The design of metaverse application in IRPS

3.1 Virtual Human

Virtual Staff. The virtual staff in IRPS can provide passengers with inquiry, ticketing, and other services through an intelligent inquiry machine, ticketing-integrated service terminals, station-integrated service desks, and other equipment. When passengers encounter problems at the station, the virtual staff in IRPS can provide remote assistance. To ensure safety, the virtual staff in IRPS also offer services on the platform, such as the location service of the train compartments and intruder alarms. The Virtual Staff in IRPS can also provide uninterrupted 24 h of service, with high stability, concurrency, and work efficiency. With the development of a front-projected holographic display, the service for locating train compartments may be replaced by this one to make the sign clearer and more prominent (Fig. 3).

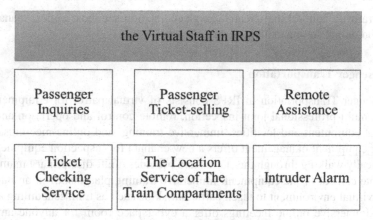

Fig. 3. The virtual staff in IRPS

Virtual Expert. The Virtual Expert of Operations in IRPS provide service that includes technology consulting, system diagnosis, regular check, failure detection, operating maintenance, automatic backup, and so on. The Passenger Service and Production Control Platform is the core of IRPS. For the knowledge base management system, the Virtual Expert of Operations provides 24-h uninterrupted maintenance services for platform users (Fig. 4).

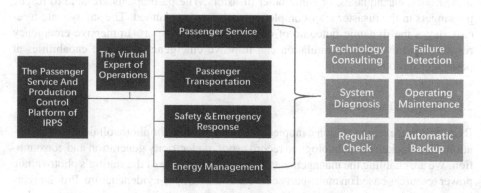

Fig. 4. The virtual expert of operations in IRPS

3.2 Passenger Service

The Passenger Service in IRPS provides Immersive navigation so that users can faster grasp the environment information, such as retail store service desk, restroom, and ticket barrier. Virtual Retail offers a new channel for buying specialty products without physically entering a store while waiting. Immersive entertainment provides interactive e-books, immersive movies and animations for children in the Baby Care Room station. Passenger extension services include cloud tourism, digital collections of railway stations, railway cultural and creative products, station sandbox games, management games, and online station exhibition galleries.

3.3 Passenger Transportation

The Passenger Transportation in IRPS consists of virtual patrol for equipment management, multi-professional joint inspection, remote control and operation and maintenance of equipment and facilities, immersive training, and online meetings. Virtual patrol for equipment management offers a new channel for inspection equipment without physically walking through the station and provides multi-disciplinary maintenance and remote control of the equipment. Immersive training places staff in an interactive learning virtual environment to teach particular skills such as train scheduling and fire-fighting. Immersive online meetings offer a cyberspace room for anyone anywhere, such as a station, train, or bureau. Participants can get their facial expressions during the conference through the avatar as if they were communicating face-to-face.

3.4 Safety &Emergency Response

The Safety &Emergency Response in IRPS consists of an immersive emergency exercise, the state prediction of security, and simulation of the emergency response and evacuation. Immersive emergency exercise offers a new way for participants to practice their skills by handling a pre-created virtual disaster such as widespread delays, fires, floods, earthquakes, or some other disasters. The participants are able to rescue passengers in the disaster after completing each step as planned. The safety state forecast shows the dynamic outcome of changes in rail transport. Immersive emergency response and evacuation simulation can improve emergency response capabilities at passenger stations.

3.5 Energy Management

By retrofitting existing station canopies and roofs to allow for photovoltaic power generation. Use blockchain technology to record proof of electricity generation and consumption. We are enabling the management of the entire lifecycle of the station's photovoltaic power resources based on multi-party consensus and tamper-evident nature. Promote carbon neutrality at railway stations. Issuance of a station passenger carbon neutral token exchange service, which rewards different amounts of tokens depending on the amount of electricity consumed, to be exchanged for more welcoming station train services.

3.6 Comprehensive Transportation Hub

As the value of digital assets continues to emerge, railway passenger stations, as data generators and holders, rely on their strengths to form station data industry ecologies. It can create a Decentralized Autonomous Organization (DAO) together with subway, air, bus, and taxi. We research the user portrait within the organization to provide accurate and personalized services.

4 Conclusions and Future Works

Based on the previous studies of Intelligent Railway Passenger Station (IRPS), we analyze the commonalities between the metaverse technology and the development direction of IRPS, and the technology architecture of the metaverse in IRPS is proposed. And we designed the metaverse application in IRPS, including virtual humans, passenger service, passenger transportation, safety &emergency response, energy management, comprehensive transportation hub, and so on. in information space to extend the temporal and spatial scale of Intelligent Railway, the metaverse technology promote the intelligent development of IRPS. But the research of the Metaverse technology is just getting started, especially in the security protection of information. We will focus on it in the follow-up study.

Acknowledgment. This work is supported by China Railway Corporation under Grants N2021X007, and the Scientific Funding for Beijing Jingwei Information Technology Corporation Limited (DZYF21-31).

References

1. Stephenson, N.: Snow Crash. Guo Z, translate. Chengdu: Sichuan Science and Technology Press, China (2009)
2. Jian, Y., Anshan, Z., Bo, P., Zhujie, B., Jiatong, L., Feiliang, W.: A review of metaverse development and its application prospect in building construction. J. Civ. Environ. Eng.https://kns.cnki.net/kcms/detail/50.1218.TU.20220602.1855.002.html. 31 Dec 2021
3. Star, X.Z., Qiao, L., Fred, Y.Y.: A review of metaverse research and applications. J. Inf. Resour. Manag. https://kns.cnki.net/kcms/detail/42.1812.G2.20220629.1127.002.html. 30 Jun 2022
4. Wenxi, W., et al.: A survey of metaverse technology. Chin. J. Eng. **44**(4), 744–756 (2022)
5. Bolin, S.: On the metaverse. Techniques of Automation and Applications **41**(06), 1–5+20 (2022)
6. Wu, G., Yang, F.: The metaverse and the "material turn" of educational practice: The old story and the new reality. Nanjing J. Soc. Sci. 135–142+160 (2022)
7. Yunwu, W., Yongzhong, W., Tengteng, W., Songxue, J., Xueting, L.: The origin, development and educational implication of the metaverse. Chin. Med. Educ. Technol. **36**(02), 121–129+133 (2022)
8. Pei-hua1, S.: Research on the Application Prospects, Main Scenarios, Risks and Challenges, Model Paths and Countermeasures of Metaverse in the Field of Cultural Tourism. Journal of Guangxi Normal University(Philosophy and Social Sciences Edition), **58**(04), 98–116 (2022)
9. Tianyun, S., Chunjia, Z.: Overall design and evaluation of intelligent railway passenger station system. Railway Computer Application **27**(07), 9–16 (2018)
10. Tianyun, S., Kaibei, P.: Overall architecture and key technologies of enhanced intelligent railway station. Railway Transport and Economy **43**(04), 72–79 (2021)
11. Jie, X., Guodong, Z., Yuanzhong, X.: Metaverse Token. China Translation and Publishing House, Beijing (2021)

Author Index

Printed in the United States
by Baker & Taylor Publisher Services

Printed in the United States
by Baker & Taylor Publisher Services